Edward E. Hale

From Thanksgiving to Fast

fifteen sermons preached in the South Congregational Church, Boston

Edward E. Hale

From Thanksgiving to Fast

fifteen sermons preached in the South Congregational Church, Boston

ISBN/EAN: 9783337264444

Printed in Europe, USA, Canada, Australia, Japan

Cover: Foto ©Lupo / pixelio.de

More available books at **www.hansebooks.com**

FROM

THANKSGIVING TO FAST

FIFTEEN SERMONS

PREACHED IN THE SOUTH CONGREGATIONAL CHURCH,
BOSTON,

BY

Edward E. Hale.

BOSTON:
ROBERTS BROTHERS, 299 WASHINGTON STREET.
A. WILLIAMS & CO., 283 WASHINGTON STREET.
GEO. H. ELLIS, 101 MILK STREET.
1879.

The Great Harvest Year.

O give thanks unto the Lord, for he is good; for his mercy endureth forever.
Who giveth food to all flesh, for his mercy endureth forever.
O give thanks unto the God of heaven, for his mercy endureth forever.
— Psalm cxxxvi., vv. 1, 25, 26.

In the earlier days of a New England Thanksgiving, the gratitude for the food which the earth and the forest have produced came foremost in all congratulations. If the wheat were blasted, if a hard frost killed the oysters for a generation, all men knew the calamity, deplored it as a judgment, and sought forgiveness. But if the harvest prospered, if the orchards groaned with fruit and the intervales with corn, if the fishermen returned early and full, all men knew that as well, and praised the God of fruit-tree, of seed-time, of harvest, and of the seas.

It is one of the notable results of a more complex social order, that now, when the national Thanksgiving Day comes round, half the people in a commonwealth like this do not know or inquire whether the harvest have been bad or good. In the compensations afforded by an eagle-eyed commerce, a hundred-fold as watchful to anticipate famine as ever Joseph was, or Pharaoh, the ordinary citizen of a town like this does not know nor care where his food comes from, to what harvest he owes it, or by what miracle it was brought to him. All he knows is that the tradesman with whom he deals sends it to his door. Is his beef from Texas or from Vermont,— he asks no question. Was his egg brought from Iowa or from Jamaica Plain,— he does not know. Is his flour from Virginia or Wisconsin,— no one has told him. He has paid for it, the grocer or the butcher has sent it, the cook has cooked it, and that is enough. Different, indeed, from the position of the fathers, for whom, if there were drought here in the Bay, it was a question almost of starvation; who, when

Thanksgiving Day came round, remembered gratefully every shower which saved the grass, and every day of sunshine which ripened the corn.

It is, indeed, to this magnificent success of Christian commerce, making such famines as those of Egypt well-nigh impossible, though we have thousands to feed where Pharaoh had hundreds,—it is to this that we owe men's indifference as to such a marvel as the harvest of this year. This harvest is so extraordinary that I have called it "The Great Harvest Year of History." But so indifferent have men become to the agencies by which they are fed, so used are the people of America to the gift of food, regarding it, indeed, as they do air or water or land, that this abundance seems taken for granted. A thousand times as much consideration has been given the question whether we ought to pay England five millions and a half dollars which the tribunal bade us pay, as has been given to that marvellous export of well-nigh a thousand millions of productions from the sale of which was created the enormous fund against which that little bill of exchange was drawn. But this ought not to be so. The myriad interchanging facilities of commerce, which make it so easy for every man to feed his household ought not to detract from our gratitude for the gift bestowed; they ought to quicken it and enlarge it.

It is not simply the cloud of Hermon which passes over thirsty Israel and makes the cliffs of Zion green. It is every mist-wreath of the Pacific, from beyond the headlands of Alaska; it is every variation of climate which has swept in from the Gulf of Mexico; it is the snow on the Rocky Mountains; it is the summer heat on the prairies of Kansas; it is the hard ice, as well, cut in your own lakes; and it is the spoil of the seas, taken by your own fishermen, which unite for the harvest: and it is God's perfect law — the law of the Power which works for righteousness — which has so far triumphed in men's affairs, that a thousand elements of blessing may thus combine for every man's welfare, and no man be left to the accidental harvest which is yielded by one or two.

Since I was made conscious last June of this marvellous miracle in progress all around us, in the unequalled harvest of the year, I have made it a matter of daily study; and I have tried to find methods of observation and of statement by which I could make clear to myself the amount of real wealth thus added to the world. But I find this very difficult, and I shall find it hard to illustrate it to you. If a man came here and told us that a hundred thousand bushels of grain were burned last night, we should be sorry. Or, if he said that a million bushels were burned, we should be just as sorry. But not more so ; for the truth is, that to most of us neither statement brings any idea of what that quantity of grain does in the work of the world,— how much life it stands for,— how many days of enjoyment, of work, of thought. The accomplished head of the commissariat of the army of the West, in 1864, told me that, at the beginning of the campaign of that year, he gave his purchasing officers in Illinois *carte blanche* to send him all the grain and corn the railroads would carry. He said that once, when Gen. Grant visited Nashville, he took him to ride and showed him his stores of corn ; and that Gen. Grant said, laughing, that, though he was an Illinois man, he did not know there was so much corn in the world. I asked how much room it took, and with some care my friend answered that it would have filled Boston Common full, to the height of a three-story house. There is the supply, say, for two hundred thousand men and their cattle and horses for a year. But think how insignificant such a supply as that is in comparison with the work which this country has had to take this year as one part, and that not the largest, of its business,— the work of feeding half the people of Great Britain ; to provide the substantial articles in the food of thirteen millions of men. The quantity which we see at any given moment seems enormous. I cannot pass so small an elevator as this on Berkeley Street, without an eager thought of more than a million homes, rich and poor, palaces and hovels, in so many lands of so many languages, which are to be fed from its abundance. But that is filled and refilled ten or fifteen times as the year goes by ; and to the dealers at the West, any one of whose great storehouses at one moment holds a year's supply for half a million men, this little elevator seems like some private granary in comparison.

The figures which try to express such a supply say coolly that in the year which ended July 1st we exported $524,000,000 worth of the productions of our farms. Of this amount speaking in round numbers, about one-third was in breadstuffs, about one-third in cotton, about one-quarter in meat and cheese. Tobacco, I am sorry to say, makes a twentieth, and sugar less than one-hundredth, of the amount. Enormous as are these sums, they only represented the harvest of 1877. So soon as the harvest of this year made itself felt, every figure was enlarged, so that the four months from July to November more than double the exports of six months before. It is idle for me here to attempt details. It is enough to say that, as this winter goes by, the nations which are relying on our surplus for substantial articles of their food, make up fully a sixth part of the human race, probably a fourth part, perhaps a larger portion.

These are products of every kind. It is our wheat or corn or barley or rice or oats or rye, or what is made from them; it is our oysters or mackerel or cod; it is our sugar or molasses or honey; it is our pork or bacon or ham or lard or mutton or poultry or eggs or beef; it is our apples or oranges or tomatoes or berries; it is our butter or our cheese,— either for the staples of life, or for the luxuries which men add to their substantial food, well-nigh a quarter part of the people of the world this day bless the United States.

And really I am sorry to have to speak of the exports first. I do so only because of these I have the figures; and there are no figures to tell of the amount of real wealth, the product of the soil, which we have here at home. It has been observed that the prices of home products are not raised by these enormous shipments. They are, on the other hand, lower than they have been for a generation. For this abundance the rich man does not care in a land where he always has enough. But to the poor man it often makes the difference between hunger and plenty. Of the matchless wealth of the most independent being on earth, the farmer who feeds with every luxury every member of his own family, almost wholly from his own farm, who shall count up the statistics? Of the similar luxury in which a great agricultural county feeds the manufacturing town at its centre, what statesman knows? Observe, then, that these shipments which feed half the world are only the surplus of our abundance, and that I named them first, not because they are the largest statement, but because they are the fullest statement which we have.

Such are the grounds for the statement I made here, a month ago, that, since the world was a world, no community of men called a nation ever gathered such a harvest as has been garnered in the United States in this year. Nor has there ever been sent from any nation such an overplus of food for the supply of the rest of mankind. The people of Rome used to send messengers to Ostia, to await the signals of the first vessels of the harvest fleet from Egypt. But the supply which that fleet brought was not more than a large week's work of this year's harvest shipments. And, when I have named that instance, I have named the largest instance in history, till I come to recent times, in which Russia has sent such enormous harvests to England and to Southern Europe. Those harvests continue enormous, but they are quite surpassed by our shipments of grain alone; and we are sending, beside, supplies of meat which more than equal in value all the Russian shipments of grain, while the Russian export of meats is in comparison inconsiderable.

It is a strange thing to say, but there are many features in this success which seem only like beginnings. I had meant to speak at some length of the humane, because intelligent, methods by which living cattle, hogs, and sheep, are transported from Boston to England, arriving, as you or I would do, the better for the voyage. This method of feeding the hungry of other lands seems wholly in its infancy, but to be growing rapidly. Our exports from Boston of living cattle have been four times larger than they were a year ago, with every prospect of a similar increase as soon as the winter has gone by; and the supply of meat sent forward in ice, of which our Northern harvest never fails, enlarges in the same wise. The same is true of the lesser articles which do not make a large figure in exhibits, but add so much to the comfort of men. Thus there has never been such export of fruit; and the market enlarges. The fish-ball, celebrated even in opera, now finds its way, ready made, to all the earth. The eggs of Iowa are sold to the cooks and confectioners of England. Moses described Palestine as a land flowing with milk and honey. But I think Moses did not dream of barges of bee-hives moving slowly up the Mississippi, so that the bees might always have fresh food, "where everlasting spring abides, and never-withering flowers,"—an arrangement which prepares the mountains of honey for lands where honey does not flow. As for milk and its products, the dairies of all America furnish milk and butter for half the nations of the world.

Am I speaking now to any idealist who has hesitated in his daily prayer, because he would not ask God for physical blessings? He would ask, he says, for more of the Holy Spirit in his heart, for more of grace, and more of love; but would not ask for daily bread, because that is the product of physical laws. I have known such men, I remember a man who would not offer the Lord's prayer, because it contained this petition for daily bread. I have known men who would not pray that pestilence may be averted, because pestilence, they said, is the result of fixed physical law, which God himself ought not to change. Am I speaking to such doubts? Let me ask that man to consider this great harvest year of history, and ask where it comes from.

What makes the harvest of this year different from that of the year when Columbus landed? Have the physical laws of the world changed? No! Have any new spiritual powers come into play? Has a living God, of constant love, directed and taught children like him? Ah, yes! He has given courage to the pioneer in Nebraska and Colorado. He has given faith to the settler's wife, that she has established in that cabin the kingdom of heaven. He has given patience, perseverance, to the wit of those inventors whose engines have reaped the harvest, and threshed it and garnered it; who have built the highways and the trains which have speeded this harvest over the land to the sea. Nay, when the men who carried on these works failed in allegiance to him and to his law, when they sought themselves first and God afterwards, then the wealth of the harvest was chaff and dust again. Witness the selfishness which last year stopped the movements of the Pennsylvania railroads for only a week; yet threatened famine thus to half a land! Witness the calamity when only one man, dishonest, uses for himself the treasure which the order of God has appointed, that in its honest use you and I and half the world may have our daily bread.

How is it that the English workman feeds on beef which a Texan drover sent to Illinois, and an Illinois farmer fattened on the abundance of the corn? Was there any natural law which compelled the ox to cross the ocean, like the fabled beast that bore Europa? Or did some steadfast man, not easily discouraged, studying in advance the problem of the feeding of the world, determine that this thing should be done? When he offered his daily prayer for daily bread, he remembered that he had no right to ask for it, unless he gave to other men theirs. And so, not of one or of two, but of ten thousand, such enterprises. And these were the enterprises of men who had faith and hope and love, the three eternal elements of life. But for these three eternities, they would neither have tried nor succeeded.

Let no man tell me that mere selfish greed sets on foot these agencies of infinite blessing. The selfish greed of the savages who ranged Nebraska never sent me a grain of wheat for my breakfast. The selfish greed of the farmers of Southern Russia never sent me one. It is not till the grace of God lifts up nations, and the men in them, to the higher law which rests on faith and hope and love, that the mountains begin to move to the sea, and the exuberance of one land to feed the necessities of another.

The prayers of men have not changed God's physical laws. They *were* well arranged when the world was set in order. But it is the prayers of loyal men — it is their work with God and his with them — which planted this continent with men who wanted to obey his law. In the midst of personal selfishness, and personal crime, the drift, the general wish, of this land has been to obey his law, as far as the land could make it out.

In that wish, the nation gives every man his homestead, in that magnificent communism which does divide the common empire among even the poorest of the people. In that wish, it gives every man his education. In that wish, it gives every man a vote. What God may work in any human heart, the nation dares not hinder. Let man work with God, and God will work with man, thirty, sixty, a hundred fold. The great harvest of to-day is the answer to prayers which we offered for a united country. It is the answer to our prayers for our brothers and sisters in the wilderness. It is the answer to our prayer for schools and colleges. It is the answer to our prayer for the freedom of the slave. It is the answer to our prayer that God will reveal himself to us, — that we may be fellow-workmen together with him. We asked him to reveal himself to his children, and the answer is in the physical blessing with which he feeds a world.

AT the end of the service of Thanksgiving Day, Mr. **Hale** read this ballad : —

THE GREAT HARVEST YEAR.

The night the century ebbed out, all worn with work and sin,
The night a twentieth century, all fresh with hope, came in,
The children watched, the evening long, the midnight clock to see,
And to wish to one another, " A Happy Century! "
They climbed upon my knee, and they tumbled on the floor,
And Bob and Nell came begging me for stories of the War.

But I told Nell that I could tell no tales but tales of peace —
God grant that for a hundred years the tales of war might cease !
I told them I would tell them of the blessed Harvest Store,
Of the Year in which God fed men as they never fed before ;
For, till that Year of matchless cheer, since suns or worlds were made,
Never sent land to other lands such gift of Daily Bread!

The War was done, and men begun to live in peaceful ways,
For thirteen years of hopes and fears, dark nights and joyful days.
If wealth would slip, if wit would trip, and neither would avail,
" Lo ! the seed-time and the harvest," saith the Lord, "shall never fail."
And to all change of ups and downs, to every hope and fear,
To men's amaze came round the days of the Great Harvest Year,
When God's command bade all the land join heart and soul and mind
And health and wealth and hand and land, for feeding half mankind.

So hot the noons of ripe July, that men took day for sleep,
And when the night shone clear and bright, they took their time to reap ;
Nor can the men cut all the grain when hungry worlds are fed,
So the ready Ruths and Orpahs are gleaning in their stead.
All through the heated summer day the Kansas maidens slept,
All through the night, with laughter light, their moonlight vigil kept ;
From set of sun the kindly moon, until the break of day,
Watched o'er their lightsome harvest-work, and cheered them on their way.
They drove their handsome horses down, they drove them up again,
While " click, click, click," the rattling knives cut off the heavy grain ;
Before it falls, around the straw the waiting wires wind,
And the well-ordered sheaves are left in still array behind.
So laughing girls the harvest reap, all chattering the while,
While " click, click, click," the shears keep their chorus, mile by mile ;
And lazy Morning blushes when she sees the harvest stands
In ordered files, those miles on miles, to feed the hungry lands.

Far in the South from day to day a living tide swept forth,
As, wave on wave, the herds of kine flowed slowly to the North.
Great broad-horned oxen, tender-eyed, and such as Juno loved,
In troops no man could number, across the prairie moved.
Behind, along their wavy line, the brown rancheros rode,
From east to west, from west to east, as North the column flowed,
To keep the host compact and close, from morn to setting sun,
Nor on the way leave one estray, as the great tide poured on.
A fair-haired Saxon boy beside commanded the array,
And as it flowed along the road, I heard the stripling say,
"'Tis God's command these beeves shall stand upon the Cheviot Hills,
The land to feed where rippling Tweed the lowland dews distills,"
So the great herd flows Northward, as the All-Father wills.

Far in the North the winter's gales blew sharply from north-west,
And locked the lakes and rivers hard in their icy rest.
I saw men scrape the crystal lakes to clear them from the snow,
I saw them drive in long straight lines the ice-ploughs to and fro;
The blocks of amethyst they slid up to the sheltering shed
By the long lines of ready rail, and as they worked they said,
"Drive close the blocks, nor leave a chink between for breath of air,
Not winter's wind nor summer's sun may ever enter there,
But square and dry and hard and smooth the ice must ready be,
When summer suns are blazing, for its journey to the sea,
To pack the meat and keep it sweet, as the good God commands,
To feed his hungry children in so many waiting lands."

And far away from Northern ice and drifts of crystal snows,
On the rich coast where deep and red the Mississippi flows,
When the thick sugar-canes were ripe beneath the autumn sun
We listened for the earliest cock to tell of day begun.
In the cool sugar-house I slept upon my pallet bed,
Where Pierre Milhet, my princely host, had called his men, and said,
"At morning's call be ready all to meet here at the mill,
That not one drop may lazy stop before the vats we fill.
What man will be the first at dawn from lazy sleep to rise,
When the first gray of daybreak pales in the eastern skies,
What man will first his load of cane fling down before the door,
For that man's wife I give as prize this old-time louis d'or."
And all day long the hard-pressed mules the heaps of ripened cane
Brought swiftly to the mill, and then rushed back to bring again,
That all day long the rollers the fresh supply might grind,
Nor should one stalk be left not gleaned on the intervale behind.
So black and white, with main and might, are all united here,
Lest the harvest lack its sweets in God's Great Harvest Year.

The boys and girls the orchards thronged, in those October days,
Where the golden sun shone hotly down athwart the purple haze.
It warmed the piles of ruddy fruit which lay beneath the trees,
From which the apples, red and gold, fell down with every breeze.
The smallest boy would creep along to clasp the farthest bough,
And throw the highest pippin to some favored girl below.
The sound hard fruit with care we chose, we laid them clean and dry,
While in the refuse heaps, unused, we let the others lie.
For pigs and cows and oxen those, for other lands were these,

And only what was hard and sound should sail across the seas.
Then, as the sun went down too soon, we piled the open crates,
And dragged them full where cellar cool threw wide its waiting gates,
So that the air which circled there was cold, but not too cold,
To keep for Eastern rivalry our Western fruit of gold.
And as old Evans thoughtful stood, and watched the boys that day,
I stood so near that I could hear the grim old farmer say,
" Shame on our Yankee orchards, if the fruit should not be good
The year the land at God's command sends half the world its food ! "

I saw what wealth untold of corn our gracious God bestowed,
As for one autumn day I sped down the Rock River Road.
All night we slept, but still we kept our tireless way till morn,
And, with the light, on left and right still stretched those shocks of corn.—
A hundred thousand girls that year wore their engagement ring,
And a hundred thousand others before another spring;
But when the husking parties came, with all their frolic play,
Those " corn-fed maidens " might have kissed and kissed and kissed all day,
And although they kissed the boys but once for every thousandth ear,
They would not kiss for half the corn that blessed harvest year.
Yet buxom girls and hearty boys were ready, as they could,
To send love's blessing with the trains that took the world its food.
For since God smiled upon his child, in comfort or in care,
Was never yet such answer made to all his children's prayer.

A north-east gale, with snow and hail, bore down upon the sea ;
With heavy rolls, beneath bare poles, we drifted to the lee.
When morning broke the skipper spoke, and never sailor shirked,
But with a will, though cold and chill, from morn to night we worked.
Off in the spray the livelong day our spinning lines we threw,
And on each hook a struggling fish back to the deck we drew.
I know I looked to windward once, but the old man scowled and said,
" Let no man flinch, nor give an inch, before his stent is made.
We've nothing for it, shipmates, but to heave the lines and pull,
Till each man's share has made the fare, and every cask is full.
This is no year for half a fare, for God this year decreed
That the forty States their hungry mates in all the lands shall feed."

Nor interval nor hind'rance the long procession break
Of the Legion which the swine-herds drive by the City of the Lake.
Up death's long way it moves all day, unconscious of its fate,
As swine with boars contend to hurry forward to the gate.
Thousands behind unwary crowd on their leaders' tracks,
Nor hesitate nor falter as they near the headsman's axe.—
For me, I stood away from blood and the silent stroke of death, [neath.
Where they packed the meat for the world to eat, in the basement crypt be-
I watched the task, as cask by cask, was rolled by stalwart men.
And car on car to travel far was added to the train ;
Nor ceased it then, but train on train pushed forth upon the rail,
Lest in some land the day's demand for daily food should fail.
For there shall not be a ship on the sea, to sail or far or near,
But the shipmates shall bless the plenteousness of the Great Harvest Year.

From last year's rice the black men the heaviest clusters choose.
And cull and thresh from every head the finest seed for use.

They beat it clean, they clayed it well, and when the field was sowed,
Up slid the sluice, and o'er the lands rushed in the waiting flood,
And then, without a ripple, above the trenches stood.
Soon through the glassy waters shot up the needles green,
With not a tare, nor "volunteer," nor choking weed between.
Then, month by month, the joints grew up so long and strong and high
That the tall men who hoed them last were hidden from the sky.
But, all the same, when harvest came, their sickles cut them low,
And they left the heads to ripen on the stubble-patch below.
From field to flats, in flats to barns, they bear the rice, until,
To thresh and beat, and clean and clear, they leave it at the mill.
The yellow husk is torn away, and the waiting casks receive
The stream of ice-white jewels from the great iron sieve.
So the black man's care sends out his share, for he knows that God has said
That his people here in his Harvest Year shall send his world its bread.

While fields were bright with summer light, and heaven was all ablaze,
O'er the broad Mohawk pastures I saw the cattle graze.
At early day they take their way, when cheerful morning warns,
And slowly leave the shelter of the hospitable barns.
The widow's son drew all the milk which the crowded bag would yield,
And sent his pretty Durham to her breakfast in the field.
One portion then for the children's bowls the urchin set away,
One part he set for cream for the next churning-day,—
But there was left enough for one little can beside,
And with this the thrifty shaver to the great cheese factory hied.
His milk was measured with the rest, and poured into the stream,
And, as he turned away, he met Van Antwerp's stately team,
Which bore a hundred gallons from the milking of that day,
And this was poured to swell the hoard fed by that milky way.—
The snowy curd is fitly stirred, the cruel presses squeeze
Until the last weak drop has passed, and lo! the solid cheese.
In Yorkshire mill, on Snowdon's hill, men eat it with their bread,
Nor think nor ask of the distant task of the boy by whom they're fed.
But when autumn's done the widow's son stands at Van Antwerp's side,
And takes in his hand his dividend paid for the milky tide.

So South and North the food send forth to meet the nations' need,
So black and white, with main and might, the hungry peoples feed;
Since God bade man subdue the earth, and harvest-time began,
Never in any land has earth been so subdued by man.

Praise God for wheat, so white and sweet, of which to make our bread!
Praise God for yellow corn, with which his waiting world is fed!
Praise God for fish and flesh and fowl he gave to man for food!
Praise God for every creature which he made and called it good!
Praise God for winter's store of ice! Praise God for summer's heat!
Praise God for fruit-tree bearing seed—"to you it is for meat"!
Praise God for all the bounty by which the world is fed!
Praise God his children all to whom he gives their daily bread!

Looking Back.

No man, having put his hand to the plough and looking back, is fit for the kingdom of God.—LUKE ix., v. 62.

The Saviour's own history, and the after-history of the New Testament, give some examples which have become proverbial. Here is poor Judas Iscariot, who bore that day the honored name of the father of his tribe,— the name which has become the name in one form of the whole Jewish nation. But Judas Iscariot, after he had put his hand to the plough, looked back, and from that hour his personal name, "Iscariot," has been the other word for "infamous"; and even the particular spelling, Judas,— because we associate it with his name,—is by common consent abandoned among men. So when poor Paul is a prisoner in Rome, he writes, sadly, "Demas has forsaken me,— having loved this present world." No man knows anything more of this wretched Demas. But to know this is enough. The name Demas stands for a "shirk." He put his hand to the plough and turned back. He is coward enough to turn from the great world of God to this petty world of things,— a man who cares for the "loaves and fishes," as in yet another application of these texts we could say. Paul himself, as one would have known, hated such people. He even broke off from Barnabas, whom he liked and loved,— who had fairly placed him in his own great place,— because Barnabas wanted to give Mark another chance. Paul could not bear to have Mark with them, because, when they came to Pamphylia, Mark slunk away, and "went not with them to the work." He put his hand to the plough and looked back.

Now such texts, and the warnings that go with them, are not to be understood as relating only to people who enlist themselves in the ecclesiastical forms of ministry,— as relating to apostles, or "the seventy," or this or that kind of evangelist, deacon, or missionary. The Saviour's statement, and the illustrations of it in history, go much farther. It is of any line of duty, of any line of ministry, as well as those which get particular ecclesiastical names; it is of furrows of all ploughing that he speaks. The boy or girl at school who finds the mathematics hard, and therefore chooses a language ; then finds the language dull, and takes another ; then drops that, and, as such people say, "takes" landscape painting; then finds he cannot "do the trees," and tries his hand at "figures"; then gives up "figures," and finds a teacher in music,—such a person shows his unfitness, not simply for literature, painting, or music, but— which is of far more importance — shows he is not fit for the kingdom of God. Such shifting change from calling to calling makes all calling mean. No duty is possible, nor are the character and dignity possible which come only from duty well performed. So grave are the warnings, and so lasting the penalties, if one be not man enough or woman enough to take brave and firm hold of the "duty that comes next his hand." That phrase is Mr. Carlyle's. If we owed him nothing else, we should owe him a great deal for saying so forcibly as he does, that no man need fret himself much about his place in life, since it is in every man's power always "to do the duty that comes next his hand." Who cannot "put that thing through," as our homely native proverb puts it,—cannot submit himself to God's purpose. God is infinite ; infinite means through, or thorough. The man who cannot "put it through" cannot "accept the universe." He cannot work by God's system. This means, in Scripture language, that he cannot save his own soul. He is not fit for the kingdom of God. " Put it through," says the proverb. It is borrowed, I think, from the ploughshare in the furrow. "Put it through!" As the Saviour says, do not turn back when you have put your hand to the plough.

I. As I meet persons really religious, I often feel that they misapprehend the relation which man's work holds to God's in daily life. There is too apt to be a theory that man is put here first of all to save his own soul; or, as another phrase has it, "to prepare himself for heaven." But the Bible statement is far better. I do not know but I repeat it here every Sunday ; but that is none too often. As early as Moses' day, inspired men saw that God put man here, first of all, to subdue the earth. That is what man is for! God called the world into being; he separated the waters from the waters; ordained light and heat; gave life to plants; and from plants evolved fishes and fowls, beasts, and, at last, man; and then the world was not finished. No! "God looked upon it," said the simple legend, "and said that it was good." Good! Yes, "very good!" But not finished. God gave it over then to man, his child, good as it was, and yet imperfect, and bade man subdue it. And that is what man is here for. He saves his own soul in subduing it. He enters God's kingdom in subduing it. But he will never make better statement of his place or his duty than that simple statement,— that for this subduing he is here at work with God.

The discovering its continents, finding out and arranging its resources, developing its physical possibilities,— that is one part of the subduing.

The seizing on its native agencies, and making them his tools, finding to the very bottom the powers of its elements,— this is another part.

The taming its living beings, the plants, the beasts,— this is another part.

Studying, discovering, and training its men and women,— this is still another, and the crowning part. The men and women are born into the world all ignorant and powerless,— of themselves. Of themselves, they grow up savages; grow up as Casper Hauser and the wild boys of the woods grew up. It is for man, who knows God's work, to train them higher, and make them more than brutes. Man finds his noblest aim in subduing the world by the interaction of social life, wheel within wheel, man acting on man, nation on nation, age acting upon age, and man all the while receiving from man, nation from nation, age from age; so that the fellow-workers with God, the children to whom he has entrusted this best work of subjugation, may become more like him and more; may, with more of Infinite Power—that is, of heavenly or spiritual power—enter on their great enterprise.

Simply, the highest work is the education of man by the interchanges of affection and of charity, of social feeling, of man working with his brother man.

So large is the variety of the fields offered to any man's choice. Such various furrows open to his plough. For such ploughing there is always a chance. From such ploughing let no man turn away.

II. Now, of this work, God himself — the "power that makes for righteousness" — is the commander-in-chief. He makes us his fellow-workmen; or we volunteer as his fellow-workmen. But it is on his plan, not ours, that the work is to be done. By that net-work of inducement, persuasion, motive, excitement, which we call Providence, every hour of every day, he assigns to you and to me, to him and to her, the thing which is to be done. "The duty next my hand," — that is the personal charge to me, given by the great commander; and to turn back from the work assigned, is not, as the careless think, to lose reward, money, or comfort, as the proverbs would teach you: far worse, — it is to lose God, because you turn away from him when you disobey him.

III. It is, however, precisely at this point that man shows that he is God's child, and not his creature merely. He is of God's nature, and is free. He shows this by his unwillingness, — possibly he shows it by his rebellion. God, "the power which makes for righteousness," hangs a rain-cloud over the garden and bids it discharge in rain, and it obeys — must obey — cannot help itself. But God brings to the garden, so watered, his own child, bids him work in the garden which is ready thus for planting; and the child does not like the duty; could be a merchant, perhaps, but does not want to be a gardener; does not choose to be a gardener for that hour; though, for that hour, he must be that or nothing. So far as he is concerned, the rain-cloud need not have been ordered, nor the seed ready for the planting. So far as he is concerned, the subduing of the earth is set back for that hour. For, in one word, it is here that there comes in the flat heresy or rebellion by which a child of God with a duty to discharge says, calmly, " I don't want to," and from that duty turns away. His hand is on the plough, and he looks back. The young nobleman looked back so. Judas Iscariot looked back so, and Mark at Pamphylia, and Demas at Rome. They are not fit for the order, method, or empire of God.

IV. Let us, then, look directly at that heresy. — "I don't want to." " Is my native genius to have no decision in this matter?" This is the frank protest of young life; insulted in its freedom to be told that another will direct its labor. "Do you say I am born to be a merchant, while he is born to be a poet, and he born to be a planter? We shall see. Rather will I wait to-day, to-morrow, the next year, if need be,— till time shall bring round the part for which I am born. For this duty next my hand, I have no genius. I shall wait, though I wait a long time, till the duty offer, to which I feel in my make-up and nature that I am born."

This protest requires solution.

Men forget that opportunity never returns while they wait, as Micawber did, for something to turn up; they forget that ability to work is the most evanescent and perishable form of property. This is what men forget when they grimly strive to starve out their employers on a strike,— what boys and girls forget when they reject this line of life or that, because it is not so genteel or so agreeable as another, or is not in the line of their genius. What I can do to-morrow between nine and twelve o'clock has certain worth, more or less, according to my aptness. But, if it is not done to-morrow, that help of mine in God's purpose is clean lost,— it is never done at all. I may do something like it Tuesday, but what I do Tuesday is Tuesday's work; and Monday's, alas! is only Monday's. It cannot by any magic be thrown over upon Tuesday. The king, in Herodotus's story, could throw his diamond ring into the sea, and, though the chances were badly against him, still it might be that a fish should catch the ring, and that very fish be brought to the king's table, and he himself open and find his ring again. But when you throw away Monday morning, there is no miracle which can bring it back to you. On that impossibility hangs all ·the gravity of labor problems. And here comes in the exceeding folly of you young people, if you are dainty in selecting the place of to-morrow's duty. In a new country like ours, twenty courses may be open. If there are, you are God's child, and you may choose between them. You may go down to Gloucester and enlist for a lay in the mackerel fleet; you may go to Colorado and go out upon a ranch to herd cattle; you may go to Florida and take up a quarter section of land there, and become a farmer; or you may train yourself for such duty by walking ten miles out of town and back again; you may answer any "Want" you find in the newspaper, or at the Industrial Aid; you may do what some young people find harder yet,— the commonplace duties at home; you may cut and split the load of wood which has come from the wharf; you may clear out the cellar; you may rake up the leaves in the garden; you may wash the windows; you may set the broken panes. Of the "duties that come next your hand," to take Mr. Carlyle's phrase again, you may make your choice. Or, of social duties, you may, any of you, write that article for the newspaper which you planned yesterday; or you can go and visit those strangers whom you resolved to visit last Sunday, and forgot afterwards. Nay, you could walk to the foot of Charles Street and go into a jail for the first time in your life, and befriend that poor fellow you find there, waiting to be summoned as a witness next January; or you could go into the children's ward in the City Hospital, and cut out some paper dolls. The choice between such appeals and possibilities is to be decided by your own fitness, your own conscience, your own genius; or, if these do not determine, even by your own whim. But all duties involve, near or distant, use for others. And when the choice is between mere selfishness for the next hour or the next day, and a duty for others,— that is, for taming the world,— why, the whole order of God demands that to that effort, at that moment, you put your hand.

The duty may be most repulsive or difficult. It may be the care of children, and you are not used to children; or perhaps a German beggar comes to you, and you cannot speak German. But it is no matter how far your taste or inclination help you, or how far your taste and inclination are mortified. The mortification may be a necessity. For till you can learn that the world has some other affairs to attend to than the rolling to and fro, *as you want it to*, there is a necessity unfulfilled in your eternal training. Till you have learned that, you cannot enter into God's order; you cannot enter the kingdom of God.

V. This appeal to steadiness concerns not only our personal duty, but some of the social questions which most perplex society.

A man's labor being the most evanescent and perishable of property, it follows that regular work, in which I can use brain and muscle and nerve every day in the year, is worth much more than spasmodic work, in which I am employed to-day and idle to-morrow. When machine-work was first introduced on shoes, I heard, to my amazement, of a contract in which some bright girls in Lynn earned four dollars and twenty-five cents a day. I remember saying that they were paid more than some excellent school-masters and doctors and ministers whom I knew. But this was not so; the girls' work ran only for three or four weeks, and they could not command the year round any such wages.

Now, the perfection of a system of work is that it shall arrange for the regular employment of this transitory force, labor, so that the people engaged may never lose a day of their time, because this day can never be replaced. Here is the reason why Essex County became such a centre of the leather trade. The fishermen of Essex County, not being used then to fish in winter, had their little shoe-shops at home, and had a winter trade as well as a summer one. Now that shoes are made the year round, fishing also has to be carried on the year round, because men cannot be unemployed. Nine-tenths of our winter poverty here in Boston comes from the modern arrangement in which the farmers of New England hire their laborers, not for a year round, but only till the end of harvest. For the winter, the farmer and his family can carry on the lesser operations of the farm, and the "hired man" drops back on us to try the resource which the lavish and more indifferent city will give to him. A certain consciousness of this lurks at the bottom of the schemes for making a day's work eight hours, or less even, by law. Add up the hours' work of all the laborers on a New England farm, and they do not amount to eight hours a day the year round. But unfortunately you cannot mow or reap or dig potatoes in January. You must work when the summer sun and the autumn harvest bid you work. And the futility of such schemes shows itself at once, therefore, when they are applied to that original work, which it is a pity we forget so often, of subduing the world in agriculture.

It followed of course, in old times, that a thrifty farmer had a well-appointed shop and tool-house, where he and his boys and his hired man spent days of blocking winter storms in cutting out fence-posts, in making gates and sleds, not to say wagons, doors, and windows; in putting tools in order, investing their own brain, nerve, and muscle, which would else be unused, in the work which else they would have to pay for from summer's labor. By the same rule, it follows that a city like ours, which has in winter to feed, directly or indirectly, some thousands of laboring men, is wise when it uses their brain, nerve, and muscle in its own workshops. This is the complete justification of the system of industry just now enlarged at Deer Island, and, on a small scale, to be set at work by the overseers of the poor in the Mayhew Schoolhouse. It is not wise for a city to undertake manufacturing in rivalry with private industry. It is wise for a city which has able-bodied men to feed, to feed them as workingmen, and not as lazy drones becoming more incompetent every day.

VI. It is to be remembered, also, that it is the laziness of those who hold back from the duty next their hands, which kills the quick and conscientious workers who are taking the places of shirks and cowards. It was the meanness of the Spartans who stayed at home which sacrificed the three hundred who died at Thermopylæ. It is said that all the work that now appears in the visible physical changes made on the surface of the world could be repeated in the next fifty years, if with the powers of modern science we could put every man to fair work in those years. It is said that all the roads and bridges, all the fences and walls, all the houses and temples, all the ships, all piers, nay, all the statues and pictures,— so far as they are physical products,— could be made in fifty years, by these thousand million men and women who will come and go in the next fifty years, if only great masters of industry could employ them as the few millions who are well employed are at work to-day. The statement seems at first an exaggeration. But when one thinks of the hordes of savages waiting on the hill-side for a flight of game, satisfied, if the game do not come, to kill a lizard or a snake and to feed upon him; when one thinks of the million men, more or less, employed last week in this country in making whiskey and rum and beer, in selling them, in transporting them, not so much as lifting a stone, or setting a peg in its place; when one thinks of strong women spending the day in making sure that the shade of a feather harmonizes with the dye of a ribbon; when one thinks of armies besieging Sebastopol, occupied for a year in skilfully destroying navies and docks which it had taken a hundred years to build; when one looks in at a club-room where he may see men of high training in the most effective nations spend all their working hours in shuffling, dealing, and playing cards, deciding whether red shall turn up or black, and on the chances staking the results of somebody's industry not their own, — one is disposed to believe the estimate. At least, one is made eager to see the great experiment tried. And one feels that the overworked men, such men as John Albion Andrew, who die too young because too much is forced upon them, are the great sacrifice we make because we choose to have only a small and compact army of well-trained workmen, while we leave at large and loose a great horde of non-combatants, who eat the rations but do not defend the lines. I preached a sermon here once in which I tried to show that the steward in the parable would not have stolen his master's money, if any man had taught him to dig. If you really want to reduce your docket of confidence-men, of peculators in high life or in low, you must see to it that boys and girls are trained honestly to the detail of duties next their hands. And while I know perfectly well that I am speaking to many persons who need to take to heart the other great gospel of laziness, — more of them are women than men, let me say in passing,— I do not know any way in which overworked men of public spirit are to be relieved from the pressure upon them, but by the inculcation of this stern gospel demand, which will relieve them in proportion as it makes all who are around them take hold and lend a hand. The ploughs will be driven easily, if no man looks back from the furrow.

Of looking back from the plough, of turning back from the work, the penalty is, that the "shirk" or coward goes out of the kingdom of God. The soul dies. Not in one or two texts, but all through, Jesus enforces work, not for God's sake but for ours. Not as if Infinite Power could not have made wheat fields bear without our work as easily as it makes daisies bloom, but because the soul of man dies out of him unless he works with God. It is work for the world, — like the work of such men as Paul and the great discoverers, like the great colonizers, the great artists, and the great teachers ; not the introspective effort of this or that meditative cloister man. "Go and do likewise." "Do even so to them." "Woe unto you lawyers who lift not these burdens." Such are the injunctions ; enough to recognize that it is in the straining of the muscles, in the positive endeavor of the mind, that the soul lives and grows. Use these tools of life, forget the soul is new-born, and it grows. Turn back to cosset it, to pet it, to brood upon it, indolent, and the very care you spend on your spoiled baby is its ruin. The young nobleman had no instruction but "Follow me." Peter and Andrew, John and James, had no call but "Follow me." Those who do follow, who do what he did, and turn to taming the world, find their souls grow to the likeness of sons of God. The multitude pressed on Christ just when he did not want them to. None the less was the multitude cared for. "As he passed by," he saw the blind man and cured him,— not when he had set out to do it. They waked him from sleep, and found he was ready. We talk of wanting to do this, and not wanting to do that! How much did he want to meet these collisions in the Temple? How much did he want the multitudes of ignorant Galileans thronging round to make him king?

If you and I have souls which are to grow, even in an infinite life, it will be by beginning, not by always getting ready to begin. It is the duty next our hand that will train us, not the waiting for some more congenial duty to appear. It is the furrow, and the work of the furrow. Woe to him who looks back! That man is never fit for the kingdom!

RITUAL.

If thou shalt seek the Lord thy God, thou shalt find him, if thou seek for him with all thy heart and all thy soul.— DEUT. iv., 29.

The eighth of January will be the seventeenth anniversary of the dedication of this church. We invite you all to meet on Thursday evening, as the evening most convenient, for a social celebration of the seventeenth birthday. And, as it is my duty, as the year begins, to collect and arrange the annual reports of your several agencies, I am going to-day a little beyond the range of their statistics to state what seem to be the principles on which public worship in our time must adjust itself, and in what directions we are to look for the improvement in our community of the administration of religion.

For those men deceive themselves who seek the perfection of worship in the repetitions of the customs of the past. The law of selection applies in such matters, as in all others. Let the Pharisees of the world, eager to copy the past, do their very best to retain customs which have no merit but their antiquity, and they fail. For instance, there has been no form of worship more universal than the sacrifice of the productions of the field upon an altar. There is no service to which history records a wider assent than this, among all tribes of men and in all periods of the world. If our business were simply to worship God, as ancient men worshipped him, it is certain that we should be bringing up the choicest fruits of our harvests; we should be driving into our sanctuaries our Texan steers, our Alderney kine, and our Narragansett sheep, and slaughtering them in token of our gratitude to God. This is the most ancient way of worship known to us, and it was at one time nearly, if not quite, universal in the world. Jesus Christ himself never said a word for the direct condemnation of it. But in presence of his indirect prohibition, before such words as, "God is a spirit, and they that worship him must worship him in spirit and in truth," all this machinery of carnage has been swept away. Strangely enough, such services have not only disappeared from Christian worship, but from Hebrew worship also, although the Hebrew contains such absolute direction, even in the nicest detail, for their regular continuance. More than this, such customs seem to have died out, or seem to be dying out, from the great religious systems of Asia ; so that you may search far and wide before you meet a traveller who has penetrated far enough into the simplicity of savage life ever to have seen a drop of blood shed in the forms of worship, or a wreath of smoke rising from the altar of sacrifice. Such a change as this means that men will adapt their religious methods to the customs of their times. The languages of religious expression grow modern just as all other languages grow modern. Prophets of Israel or Pharisees of the later days, like our antiquarians of to-day, will stand upon their high cliffs by the seashore and shout out to the men in the boats that they must not drift upon the tide. But all the same the flood carries them along, and the prophets and the Pharisees and the antiquarians must e'en trudge after them along the sands ; must take up a new position, and will there again advise them to stand by the customs of antiquity. That position they will abandon in its turn, and meekly follow after the tide.

Failing thus to retain the facts of old-time worship, the antiquarians of religion, whom Mr. Whittier calls the "backward looking sons of time," try a half-way policy, by way of conciliation, and introduce symbols of the customs which time so ruthlessly abandons. Take the worship in the city of Rome to-day, as compared with the worship in the same city in the second and third centuries. The faithful in that early time were jealously watched by spies, people of the grade whom we now call "detectives," and their meetings for worship were prohibited, even under the most humane emperors. They devised ways, therefore, of doing that under ground which they were not permitted to do above ground. Under whatever pretext. men, women, and children strolled away from their homes, and when they were sure they were not watched crept into the dark passages of the underground catacombs by which the site of that city is honeycombed beneath the surface. Where two or three of these passages meet, a little room is made,— never large, of course, because the frail stone of the roof has no other columns to support it than the rough masses which the quarry-men have not cut away. In such a cavity a little body of Christians would meet to say their prayers, to sing their hymns, to pass from hand to hand a bit of bread or a cup of wine. And when, in time, these crypts became the places of their burial, the sarcophagus in which some body lay, a block of stone hewn out and covered with a slab, became fit place for the candles which lighted the vault, and for the cups and plates which contained the wine and bread. Here is the reason why in the service of the Roman Church to-day a distinguished sanctity is given to a stone altar in shape of a tomb, and why lighted candles burn in the day-time for worship and for festival. Of course one understands how such a custom may be clung to, as mere matter of preference or fancy. But when you find that every Catholic church in the world must have an altar in that shape because a few thousand Roman Christians, a very small fraction of the Church of their day, happened to worship so, you are amazed that a relentless fancy can be pushed so far. And when you see high officers of the English Church fairly at feud, and even going to law, about the shape of these altars and the lighting of these candles, you see that such antiquarians of to-day are, like the Pharisees of the old centuries, "backward looking sons of time," fighting in vain to keep an ancient language in memory. Granting that while in Rome, if the Church wanted to retain a memorial service in the ancient crypts it might do so, it seems as if an angel of light would say that for the Church at large, the Church of the wider world, the special business of to-day is to proclaim that it is not under ground as some of the fathers were. It walks in the light and is no longer sentenced to darkness. It controls the powers of the State and fears them no longer. Far from clinging to mere memories of darkness and the tomb in its ritual, one would say that the true ritualist would devise for the Church every expression of that joy to all people for which the Church was established; which in its triumph it has already won so far.

I have no wish to base an argument on an individual instance. As you know, I could adduce a thousand illustrations. They would all teach the same lesson, — that religion, like every other interest in life, must use the language that people understand. "Dark parables, — owned as truths of old," — as the hymn calls them, are all useless for the religion of to-day, unless somebody unfolds them. As Paul says, in his resolute way, "I had rather speak five words in the Church with my understanding, that I might teach others also, than ten thousand words in an unknown tongue." One would like to know what a church says to that, which repeats its prayers in the Latin language to-day, — or a church whose symbolism of dress and of other costume is so ancient that it needs a cyclopædia to explain it to those who look on.

There is of course a reaction from such formality. It shows itself in such plans as those of the Society of Friends, — "the people called Quakers," — in their effort to dispense with all forms. Thus architecture becomes oppressive in its requisitions, as when an architect builds a church where no voice can be heard; and the Quaker protests, by leaving off steeple and other adornment, and making of his house a mere meeting-house. So baptism and the Lord's supper are encumbered with superstition; and the Quaker omits them. Or a stated priesthood becomes the nurse of formality; and the Quaker dispenses with a stated priesthood. The experiment is magnificent for its courage, and it is very instructive. Alas, the most distinct lesson from it is, that a new set of forms come in at the window where another has been put out at the door. Thus, in the rapid simplifying of class costume, the dress of the Friends, meant to be so simple, is now the only distinguishing costume left to us but that of the army. And no intonations of Romanists or Anglicans are so distinctly marked as the cadences of a Quaker preacher. To hold to the custom of the seventeenth century is as fatal as to hold to that of the fifth or of the tenth; and this the loyal experiment of the Friends has taught us.

The New England Congregationalists, of whom we are, tried experiments not dissimilar. They are well enough illustrated by a habit trivial in itself, by which we New-Englanders once left out all cheerfulness, all color, from the adornment of our houses. I remember that forty years ago, — in real inability to decorate our rooms intelligently, — we satisfied ourselves with drab walls, white ceilings, and the ugliest mouldings, if they were only "plain." That is a good enough type of a habit of worship in which preachers addressed God as they would never dare to address either a friend, or a judge, or a sovereign. In the same habit they read hymns so absurd that they would have scouted them in a newspaper, and sang tunes in church which would never have been permitted in a concert room. All this belonged to the determination to avoid all superstition in service, and this left them virtually with a service which came to be called "preaching," or perhaps "meeting,"— so thoroughly was all notion of worship beaten out of it.

Now it is perfectly true that each generation will infallibly omit many of the rites of the past. Just as we do not speak Anglo-Saxon or Gaelic, just as our other language has been modified, the language of our worship is modified from generation to generation. And it is not hard to see what are to be the lines of the methods of worship of the future.

The Church must have ritual,— which expresses the brotherhood of man ;

Which gives opportunity for common worship;

Which shall be large and generous ;

Which shall be the worship of people as of minister ;

Which shall be elastic ;

And at the same moment it must be, when necessary, the grandest expression possible of men's faith and hope and love.

Let me speak of these points in their order.

1. Ritual must express communion or brotherhood. The old architectural rule was that the floor of a church must be on the level of the outer street. The architects meant that the church was in no sort raised above the needs of daily life. We dispense with that outward form, if need be. But we must not dispense with the thing. Thus doors to pews are bad ritual, because they seem to mean exclusion. High pew divisions are bad ritual. In Christopher Wren's churches there were partitions so high that people could not look from pew to pew. This was because in Charles II.'s time people did not believe in human brotherhood, and might well be unwilling to see some of their neighbors. But to maintain such divisions in a church is bad ritual. It is good ritual to meet a stranger at the door and lead him at once to a seat. It is the worst of ritual to tell a man that he has your seat and must leave it. It is good ritual to be on the lookout for an exceptional person, as a black man, or a ragged woman, or a person whose aspect is foreign, and to make him feel at ease. The whole service from the beginning must show that we are children of one blood and engaged in one purpose.

2. Ritual must give opportunity for common worship. When we read the psalm it is good ritual for all to read,—to read slowly and with the heart. A congregational hymn sung with life and spirit is admirably good ritual. So it is good ritual when the whole congregation is in church at the beginning of the service. It is bad ritual when they trail in, in long succession, as if they had doubted whether they would come at all. It would be good ritual again, if we could so

overcome our timidity here as to unite in the Lord's Prayer. It is bad ritual when the minister uses in prayer such phrases as the congregation would not use, or language which the simplest person would not understand. Nor should he ever offer petition at a venture. If he prays for the sailor, it is because he remembers a sailor; or for the sick, his heart is with that darling girl or that dear old man. If he offer any expression merely because it is in the Bible or in a prayer-book, that is the worst of ritual. When a sympathetic choir takes up the reading of a prophecy with a strain of it which Isaiah would have rejoiced to hear, there is good ritual. When a minister is correcting the notes of his sermon while the choir is singing a hymn, his ritual is very bad ritual.

3. Ritual must never be small or mean, hurried or apologetic; people must never carry it through as something of little consequence, which is to be got out of the way. I have heard people call the worship of a church "the introductory exercises." The newspapers are too apt to call them so. The truth is that the worship is what we come for,— the sermon is an accident or incident, not essential. Yet I never go down town but I see two or three signs, on as many chapels, saying that "preaching" is at such a time. One guesses that those signs are ordered by the minister, and that he thinks more of himself than of the God who calls the worshippers together. If the service is only the taking an oath in court, the dignity of the method should show that the Infinite Being is in that little company. I hear people talk as if congregational ritual were of its nature jejune or unadorned. Congregational ritual need not even be simple, though there are always advantages in simplicity, and there are dangers in a complex service. But really, where, as in a Congregational church, a thousand persons, all of whom are priests and kings, unite in praise, prayer, or penitence,— the service ought to be certain to be grand and dignified. When — as in a hierarchical church — one feeble man bears the prayers and penitence of the thousand,— is their intermediary and prays for them,— why, then there is excuse, if a fit of illness, if a fever or a headache, render him unfit for the solemnity; if his expression be mechanical, and even his devotions cold.

4. This is the reason why good ritual requires signs of union by the people with their minister, and why signs of it are always so gratifying. In the war, I was speaking here once of the work of the Sanitary Commission. A young officer, on leave of absence, said to me afterwards, "I was

tempted to rise and tell how, in North Carolina, their supplies arrived two days in advance of the government stores, and were untold blessing to wounded men." "Tempted!" I cried; "and why did not you? Just such expression is the right of every member of the congregation, when, as here, the end justifies the interruption." In the Hebrew worship, seven laymen come in turn from the congregation into the pulpit, and read their parts of the Scripture. This is perfect ritual. It shows, in living fact, that this minister is a man, and that these men are ministers. In one of the most elaborate churches of the "high church" in England, I saw the same thing. When the minister came to the Old Testament lesson he beckoned to a gentleman in the congregation who was not a priest, who read that part of the service.

5. When I say ritual should be elastic, I mean ritual which can be readily adapted to the immediate exigency. I can illustrate what I mean by two personal anecdotes.

I was in Washington in the second year of the war, at a period of great depression of feeling there. It was my duty to preach, and the committee of the church came to me, and asked me to arrange a vesper service in special reference to the needs of some families who were in great sorrow. They had lost near friends in battle, or in more instances they were in daily attendance in the hospitals, and were saddened by the suffering and death of the patients in their charge. I made all the preparation for such a service. I remember that the people were to read with me the psalm: "Why art thou cast down, O my soul, and why art thou disquieted within me?" that the Scriptures I had selected to read were for an occasion of mourning, and that all three of the hymns were chosen for the same purpose.

After this preparation, I was the first person to enter the church before the service. I sat alone in the pulpit, unable to see any of the congregation. Of a sudden the sexton came to me, with a note from the leader of the choir with whom I had arranged this funereal service. The note read:—

"We have taken New Orleans, and we shall sing Te Deum."

The news was immediately confirmed. By his promptness only was I saved from giving out such hymns as,

"Oh, help us when our spirits bleed,"

to be sung by an immense jubilant congregation; and from

asking them to read, in expression of their feeling of triumph: "Why art thou cast down, O my soul, and why art thou disquieted within me?"

Warned in time, I changed every part of the arrangement of the service. We sang three hymns of thanksgiving for mercy to the nation. We read together one of the psalms of thanksgiving. That congregation had never before united in a responsive service, but every man and woman read with unction and spirit when we came to the passages:—

"Who slew mighty kings; for his mercy endureth forever.

"And gave their lands as a heritage; for his mercy endureth forever.

"Even for a heritage to Israel his servant; for his mercy endureth forever."

You can see how glad I was that our elastic congregational ritual enabled me to change all the rest of the service as readily as I changed my address. You can guess how glad I was that we were not obliged to express the joy and gratitude of an immense congregation in a form selected three hundred years ago for the third Sunday before Trinity.

On another occasion, also in the period of the war, I preached in the same church when we were to celebrate the communion. Some event of national triumph, I have forgotten what, had crowded the church. My address before the administration of the supper was very short; and when I left the pulpit that large assembly, called together as they were under some special impulse of gratitude, all remained without moving. No one left the church before the communion service. It happened, therefore, that when the officers of the church took the bread and the wine from my hands and distributed those emblems, they had not passed a quarter way down the aisles before paten and chalice were empty; and so they returned them to me. What emblem more perfect of the universal interest and gratitude of that throng! How glad was I again that the elastic ritual of a congregational church did not compel me to interrogate any man as to his right to bread and wine, or to pretend that those had not communed who had failed to receive a crumb of one or a drop of the other.

6. Ritual must never be petty nor apologetic. It must be grand because its purpose is infinite. I claim for congregational ritual, when it is true to the great principles involved in congregational worship, that it is more capable of the grandest expression than is any other method of service. For instance, the noblest service of worship in which I ever joined, whether in our own churches or in the cathedrals of

Europe, was our own Thanksgiving service here on the afternoon of the third of February last, when we commemorated the goodness of God to our church in half a century. I think you will all say the same thing. What made that service so noble? It was that an immense congregation, who had come with one special purpose and knew what that purpose was, united in it. Not a person here but had come for that commemoration.

The worshippers were also completely in earnest. There was no question in their minds. They were glad that the church had passed through fifty years of prosperity, and had a chance for fifty years more. More than this, they were disposed to give God the praise. Now, to voice that praise they were not condemned to a Collect for Thanksgiving, written three centuries ago, and fitted for all possible occasions of gratitude,— which is to say, precisely fitted for no one. To voice that praise, in the freedom of our ritual we were able to use that matchless "Song of Praise" which one of the inspired masters composed for the fit celebration of one of God's greatest gifts to men. Better than this and more,— we had only to ask, what no man could command, and we had the hearty and glad assistance of thirty or forty of the most accomplished musicians, who came to us as glad as we were to render to God, for once, a fit tribute of human gratitude for this sleepless tenderness of his, in which alone the plans of men succeed. No one who was here that day will ever forget that service of gratitude. From whatever level of thought or anxiety, the strains of music and the sympathy of faith lifted us to the level of glad rejoicing. We began the new half-century of our existence as a church on a nobler level for worship and for life. We had given thanks to God in an expression grander than the concert room could achieve,— utterly beyond any mere technical formality, whether of fine art on the one side, or of rubric on the other. We had brought our very best to the Most High.

Observe now that such an expression of praise, as a part of public religious service, would have been impossible in any church but one which enjoys the elasticity of congregational ritual.*

Of all degradations of worship, the basest is the pretence of devotion you do not feel. I never saw a face so sad as

---

* It is indeed curious that, although the religious habit and taste of England may almost be said to have devised the "oratorio," as a separate class of sacred music, it is only in the rarest exceptional instances that any of the great oratorios are heard in England, in an English church, — or, indeed, outside of a concert room.

that of a priest in the Cathedral of Mayence, who had to repeat the Lord's Prayer thirty-five times in a little more than an hour. This is in a service which is called a "Thirty" or a "Triginta" from this frequent repetition. I stood near enough to the poor fellow to see the almost agony of his face, as he forced himself, as well as he could, into thought and feeling; and I saw also, or thought I saw, his terror lest the function should become mechanical. Now this danger is quite as much the danger of the congregation as of the minister. This poor man was chained in that mechanical order of the most mechanical hierarchy. He must say the Lord's Prayer thirty-five times, as a sentinel in a garrison must pace five hundred times on such a beat. And you, when you come to church, — how great is the danger that the service falls into routine! You were here last Sunday; you will be here next Sunday. You sat in that very place; you held this very psalm book — nay, it seems as if the minister spoke these very words. All these temptations run in the way of drowsy devotion, of mechanical worship, — not lifted by enthusiasm, nay, not informed by thought. It is against these temptations that we must strengthen ourselves, even before we enter here. To put away resolutely yesterday's annoyances and petty perplexities; to recall — yes, and to arrange in order, — last week's causes for gratitude; to determine what one most needs from God, and, even as one walks to church, to ask him for it in unspoken prayer; to forgive, and that forever, whatever man or woman has been mean, or sly, or otherwise bad to you; to enter thus the house of God, calm, cheerful, ready for the meeting with God in prayer, — this is to make sure that the service shall be real for you, and not a thing of routine. A man who goes every week-day to his store, resolved and certain that every letter shall be answered, every order filled, every obligation met, ought to know how to come here on Sunday, not as to a form or for a recreation, but with a like resolve that every purpose of Sunday shall be fulfilled before he leaves this house. As he would not take a novel to his counting-room, so he will not bring here his petty daily perplexities. As he devotes himself to his duty in his store, so he devotes himself here to glad worship, to prayer and to praise. It is to such devotion that an answer is promised.

"If ye seek me, surely ye shall find me, when ye shall seek for me with all your heart."

The next sermon in this series will be a sermon on Prayer.

4

PRAYER.

The publican would not lift up so much as his eyes unto heaven, but smote upon his breast, saying, God be merciful to me a sinner.— LUKE xviii., 13.

I spoke here last Sunday of that dread of the Bible — amounting sometimes to hatred of it — which is bred by the mechanical idolatry of the Bible,— very naturally bred,— and to be removed only by more rational use of it.

Kindred to this dread, and bred from like training, is the distrust of prayer to which people come who have been trained in the mechanical schools of what is called religion. Nothing is more pathetic than the courageous confession of this distrust. People come to consult you: "What is true, and what is not true?" Then, when you say that any real life of the soul, though it be bold inquiry, is of course more pleasing to God than any dead acquiescence in mechanical assertion, people take confidence enough to confess the bitterest doubt of all: ·"But you do not know," they say, "how far I have gone; for I am so wretched, or I am so confused, or I am in such doubt, that I do not pray. I have lost my confidence in prayer."

Now certainly I do not expect to restore that confidence by anything I can say in half an hour. I would as soon try to make the root of a rose-tree throw up a new stem, and make that stem bud and throw out leaves, and from the shelter of the leaves throw out another germ of finer quality, which should end in a flower-bud which should open into a rose,— I would as soon do this, in the space of half an hour, by talking about it. But in less than half an hour I can show what it is that deadened the rose-bush; and in less than half an hour I can show what is the mechanical handling of spiritual themes, from which such unspiritual distrust has grown. I can, I think, show the exceeding rashness of trying "to describe the indescribable," and to measure the immeasurable. It is from this rashness that the distrust we deal with chiefly springs.

For people choose to talk — I am sorry to say they choose to preach — as if they had peered into every corner of the universe; had been God's prime counsellors ever since eternity began, and before. They choose to talk as if the prayers of a few of the elect, on this world alone, are the only appeals addressed to what we call, stupidly enough, his wisdom, his justice, his foresight, and his love. You would suppose that he were chained at some distant bureau, where our prayers are put on file, docketed, and attended to, and where nothing else is attended to. This is bad enough. But, worse than this, they talk as if prayer were simply petition; nay, worse than petition, — as if it were only beggary. It is as if we, all alien from him and all unlike him, impotent of ourselves, and dying without him, had still to persuade him, all unwilling to be persuaded, nay, even to force or to purchase him, by the importunity of our petitions. It would really seem, from what you hear sometimes, as if, in the parable of the unjust judge, the judge were intended by the Saviour to represent the character of God himself. But in truth, the whole force of that parable turns, as in the other kindred parable, on the moral, "If a father or judge so fallible and so hard, — if he answers our appeals, how much more our Infinite Father whose name is Love!"

I. Low down in all this mechanical conception of prayer is the mistake which supposes that the chief object of prayer is solicitation, or what I called beggary. Among the mistakes in this matter, I regard this as the fundamental mistake.

And from this mistake all the worst difficulties and misconceptions spring. Prayer is not beggary. It is intercourse between the child and father. "Communion" is probably the best name we can give to it, if we are so scientific that we must have a name in which the etymology expresses the whole idea. The thing itself is perfectly expressed on the door-step of a happy home, when the father and mother come back after a little absence. A group of children have caught sight of the carriage in the distance, and come tumbling round them to express their joy that the companionship which has been broken is resumed. If you must explain in long words a thing in itself so real, and which needs so little explanation, — here it is: "The companionship which was broken is resumed." Do those children ask for anything? Maybe they do, maybe not. If the father has been in the habit of bringing at such times a toy, an apple, a book, the smaller children will ask for it, or will search his pockets for it. But the larger children will be ashamed, and will tell the little ones that they must not tease him. They know that real affection does not ask unless there is real necessity. And the main-spring of the life of the occasion is not petition; it is not begging. It is joy that those who have seemed to be parted are again together.

Now all this may be said, without change of words, of the prayer of children to their God. I have found it indeed difficult to describe this interview in other words than those in which we describe prayer. It is interesting to notice how much the very best hymns of all ages have of the genuine feeling, and how little of beggary. Take "Nearer, my God, to Thee," which is a prayer through and through. You would hardly call any wish there expressed a petition. Looking at the best hymns, I may fairly say that petition is not their chief object. There will be the acknowledgment of God's power, there is implied the weakness of the child; and then, perhaps, the child asks for health or peace or life. This is because the child is child, and prays to the Father, whose nature he partakes; he asks for more of the life of God, of the peace of God, and that supreme health which comes only where this life and peace have come.

II. But if asking or begging is not the chief good of prayer, what is the good of it? That question is seriously asked. Once more we must accept the analogies of other intimacies or intercourse. "What is the good of it?". Have we, then, reduced all society to an interchange of values,— to buying and selling? When I ask my friend to walk with me, is it understood that I am to give so much information before we return, and that he is to pay me with so much amusement? When, in the evening, two or three friends come in on me for an hour's visit, must I understand that they have come with a purpose of so much to be got out of me? Is there always a hidden "axe to grind," as the heathen say? Is this visit of theirs a transaction which may be posted on the ledger,— DR. so much good-sense on one side, CR. so much entertainment on the other? When, after a long term, the tired school-boy hurries home by the first train, revelling in the prospect of so many weeks with brothers and sisters, father and mother, is it only because his sisters will teach him to dance, and his brothers will teach him to swim; because his mother will bake a cake for him, and his father kill the fatted calf for him? Are we so utilitarian as to have degraded thus to a something for something the whole charm of love, of friendship or society?

No! All these associations come in, of course, to human beings, because they are of one life, of one soul, of one heart, and of one mind. They are of one nature, and they cannot help showing it if they would.

Yes! And just so the child seeks his Father,— nay, why should I not say the Father seeks his child,— because they are of one nature, of one life, of one soul, of one heart, and of one mind. The child is born from the Father, and he cannot help showing it if he would.

It will of course happen, and I wish we could always remember, that language will fail us terribly,— sometimes it fails completely,— in the effort of man, the child, to speak of infinite love to God, the father. But this is not the only strain in which language fails; and when we say or feel that words are not sufficient,— is not this what every one complains of so soon as he tries to speak of his love in words, or indeed of any other passion? It is curious to see that in one age men give up the experiment of words and try the experiment of actions, in the hope of drawing nearer God; and then in another age they give up the experiment of action, and try the experiment of words again. The whole system of Moses is founded on the natural effect of sacrifice. The shepherd brings his lamb, the farmer brings his wheat, to the altar, that, by giving up a part of the harvest, he may show his gratitude to the Lord of all the harvest. But when, in time, such songs as David's are sung,— "The Lord is my Shepherd; I shall not want"; or, "Oh, my God, my heart is cast down within me,"— the spoken word seems to bring the child nearer than the material sacrifice. So in time, at last, some poet makes God say, "If I were hungry I would not tell thee, for all the beasts of the forest are mine, and the cattle upon a thousand hills"; and thus in time the system of visible sacrifice, with the false asceticism connected with it, has a weaker hold; and we say truly that, though the Saviour never condemned it, it died out under the words, "God is a Spirit." There has been, from the day those words were spoken, no burnt offering, or first fruits of the field, offered on Christian altar. Men bring, instead, their prayers and hymns,—what Hosea calls in his prophecy "The calves of their lips," for their communion. But in time, words also in their turn will become rusty, and heavy, and dead. What is so dead as a liturgy that has lost its meaning in endless repetition, like the heathen's? The Tartar's prayer, upon a turning board whirled round a hundred times by a manipulator, is not more wooden. And so, in course of time, you shall hear the reversed complaint. Men begin to say that words part them from the Spirit whom they seek. They quote the old monk: "*Laborare est orare,*"—to labor is to pray. They recall such words as Zoroaster's, as we heard it last Wednesday evening,—that he who digs in the ground comes nearer God than he who offers prayers in words, and does no more. Our own time is, perhaps, in the mood to repeat this protest, which is, indeed, nowhere stated more bitterly than in the Sermon on the Mount, in its guard against wordy prayers, —

"When ye pray, use not vain repetitions, as the heathen do, for they think they shall be heard for their much speaking."

But neither of these protests—that against forms of sacrifice or forms of language — has anything to do with the essence of prayer. For prayer may be without sacrifice and without language ; it is simply the conscious wish to draw nearer God. The man who labors in the field does pray, if the object of his labor is that he may come nearer God; the priest chanting his Latin anthem prays, if the object of his anthem is that he may come nearer God. If the man works in the field simply to feed his family, or to sell his crop, he does not pray ; if the priest chants merely because it is so ordered in the office, he does not pray. And the publican who beat upon his breast because he sought God prayed ; he would have prayed in that beating of the breast, though he had not spoken the words, "God be merciful to me a sinner."

III. The child appeals to the Father; now does the Father show that he is conscious of the child's appeal ?

Ah ! here is the question of questions !

It is on this question and the answer to it that the people who worship in the world are parted from those who do not worship ; and that, in practice, the people who are without God in the world are parted from those to whom God is a present Friend.

It is not, indeed, largely a question for argument ; it is a question of experience or of fact, and the matter is one where the experience of one person is only in a limited degree helpful to another.

The universal instinct of mankind, undoubtedly,— seeing the amazing power in all the universe, seeing the sweep of the winds, the havoc of the waves, the soft and gentle empire of the sun — leads each man and woman and child to cry out to this Power in his own weakness, and to invoke its help. Out of this instinct have been builded all temples, and have grown up all institutions for worship.

It is just in proportion as men have learned that that Power in all the universe is larger than their fathers thought, that it rules regions vaster than thought, indeed, by agencies inconceivable,— it is just then and there that the men who have found this out, are staggered by the sense of their own littleness in comparison, and that they say, "It is impossible that I, so slight, can speak a word which shall be heard, or known, or cared for by a Force which is so overwhelming." It is just here that there comes in that practical atheism which supposes that God does not listen to, or is not conscious of, his children.

In the line of argument, as I said, not much is to be said in this appeal. But the analogies of the relations of little and great, even of the very little to the very great, are all the other way.

The orbit of a comet may be an infinite Hyperbola. That is to say, it may extend outside the system of this world, and cross the system of all worlds on a curve which we know never returns into itself. Still we calculate the law of that orbit, by what is called its differential. By this we mean a fragment of it which is infinitely small,— which is confessed to be infinitely small. It is so small that it cannot be put upon paper. If it could be, the calculation would be void. Now no man of science, and no man of sense, who knows anything of what he talks about, says therefore, that it is impossible that the little differential shall be reckoned a part of the infinite orbit, or as having vital connection with it.

No! For this would be to say that the little spark may be so small that it cannot fire the great magazine; that if it were only a cartridge it would be possible, but that to light a magazine,— that were impossible. This "little and great" heresy cannot come in, except in utter confusion of what is easily confused,— the relations of finite with infinite.

This is to say, all science shows that between little and great there is no real or essential distinction. The distinction is a name applied by us who look on, describing our place in the system rather than any essential difference between parts of the system. The microscope, revealing what we call infinitely small, goes as far in its disclosures as the telescope goes, revealing what we call infinitely great. And at each end of this scale we find the same law. The higher mathematics all start from the certainty that what is infinitely large may be stated in the laws obtained by the study of a part of a curve infinitely small. And this law, which the hymn states correctly when it sings,—

> "To Thee there's nothing old appears,
> O God, there's nothing new,"

may be stated as correctly in saying,—

> To Thee there's nothing great appears,
> O God, there's nothing small.

A word rightly spoken, at a supreme instant of time, may change all history forever. One thought, at one happy flash of what we will call inspiration, may change philosophy, and religion, and society forever. Not Christianity only, but all that we know of life or of law, agrees in this: that one and the same Life controls the universe, and that the law of this Life knows no control by size or by quantity. It is as perfect in the smallest moon of Mars as it is in gigantic Jupiter. It is as perfect in the speck of the sunbeam as it is in the sun himself, or as it is in the system of systems of which the sun himself is a speck in turn.

The analogies, indeed, all confirm the voice of the universal instinct, which has built temples that outlasted every structure of art or of arms; which has sung words which have outlasted every word of other love or of other poetry; the instinct indeed of human nature, which has a right to say that thus far time has not weakened it. But the real decision of this great central question is not a matter of the analogies, but of experience,— of personal experience; it is a part of the solemn experience of a man's own life.

So far as history goes, it will be confessed that those men who yield to the instinct of worship, who seek God with all their hearts, find him. They think they find him, and say they find him. They, too, might have said it was impossible he should care for them; they, too, might have said it was impossible to obtain an answer. So the boy on the beach is very apt to say it is impossible for him to keep afloat upon the sea. And this is very certain: that unless he, too, trust himself, yes, again and again, to the waves, he will never swim upon them; he will never play with them; will never rise and fall on their swelling and receding; will never float motionless upon their surface. If he cannot trust them they cannot serve him. So it is very certain that the men without heart or courage, who say it is impossible for God to care for them, and impossible for them to gain an answer to their prayer, can never know what such answer is. No! They cannot conceive of it. But those other men, who knew they were little and yet had so much of infinite being in them that they were willing to trust that which is great, who seek God with all their hearts,— they find him; they say they find him. That is the verdict — the unanimous verdict — of the history of such men. Not but there are many men who have gone through forms of devotion, and have fallen back dissatisfied; many men, too, who have asked for this crumb or that loaf, and have not received it, and so have refused to ask for another. But no men and no women have left it upon record that, in the secrecy of daily or hourly communion, they have unfolded to God every secret, have thanked him for his favors, have tried to open life to his quickening, and have listened to know what he had to say to them, but they have also declared that, after such self-surrender, fairly persisted in, in joy and in sorrow, in courage or in doubt, they have been more alive, — they have found the heavens open, and knew the present Father's love!

Not one of them all has found the heavens adamant, or says that no answering strength has come to the longing spirit. Not one!

IV. We are, of course, to guard ourselves against the intricacies,— shall I say the absurdities? — whether of enthusiasts or of machine-builders, who undertake to decorate and amplify, and who distort the simple office of prayer in a thousand heathen repetitions. We can have no censure for the ridicule heaped deservedly on such verbiage or upholstery. God is a Spirit; and we, his children, so far as we pray to him, are spirits also. Our prayer, then, is to be of the very simplest. It is the honest effort of the spirit of the child to find out — shall I say to signalize or telegraph? — the Infinite Spirit from which it is born. All offerings of sheep and oxen, of turtle-doves and pigeons, of incense and costume, of adjectives and adverbs and interjections, may well be seen to vitiate and chill effort so august because so simple.

What is this effort, then, in its august simplicity? What is the expression of the child, and what answer shall he have from the Father? Of course there is no likeness with which it is to be fully likened. The constant failure of parable or illustration must appear. But love is always infinite; so that any display of love anywhere will help us, though it furnish only an inadequate analogy.

A tired child is leaning on her mother's shoulder, as they ride at night. She is too tired to sleep. And her mother does not sleep. To the poor girl everything seems as dismal as it is dark, except this blessed certainty that her mother is here. Must she speak to her, to say so? No! Neither of them needs that. Must she ask her mother for anything as a sign of love? Why no! To suggest that is absurd. But as she lies there, happy in the sense of this unfailing sympathy of her mother's heart,—happy, if you please, in the certainty that this mother understands her, understands all her gropings and strugglings,—as the tide of this happiness rises to the full, she must do something to express it, and she just presses upon her mother's hand with the finger that clasps it. And her mother,—she says nothing, she asks nothing; she knows all that this pressure means, and she returns it in the same way.

Now, if one must condescend to what seems almost the blasphemy of analyzing that tie between mother and daughter and its expression, it means this: The child means, " Dear mother, I love you with all my heart, and I know that you love me." And the mother means, " Dear child, I love you with all my heart, and I know that you love me." The child means, " Dear mother, I should be perfectly wretched in this dismal darkness if I were quite alone; but on your breast I am perfectly happy." The mother means, " Dear child, if I thought I were alone, and had not you to live for or love, I should be perfectly wretched; but, knowing that you love me, I am perfectly happy." To express this from each to each, the throb of a little finger is sufficient. When it has been once expressed, they rest still, if you please, for a moment; but the turn comes again,—the certainty of communion is too exquisite to be refused. And again in one signal the child tells the mother everything, and in the same signal receives everything from a mother's love.

Now that child and mother could say no more — would not say so much — if the child wrote out a copy of verses to express her feeling, and, in ribbons and satins, with the pomp of a French solemnity, presented the offering to her dear mamma. And, on the other hand, no argument would demonstrate to the child that she had no answer from her mother because there was no visible token, no oracle that she could repeat, or no offering that she could show.

We analyze in like fashion the old Greek hymns and the liturgies; and we say: " 'This is ignorant," "That is heathen," "This other word is selfish." Perhaps they are. But our question is not, whether man, who prays, is childish, whether he is heathen, ignorant, or selfish. It is, whether he have been all wrong in his determined notion that with the Force or Power that rules the universe he can converse or no. What we need to learn is, that this conversation is not in thunders or in lightnings, but in the still, small voice,— where Elijah found it, where the Saviour heard it, as this happy child finds it who is resting in her mother's arms.

For that discovery will adjust for us all the uncertainties and doubts about the method of our prayers. Two of you who are brothers are parted by the ocean; but you are able to arrange that at a moment fixed — shall I say a blessed jubilee Sabbath of your lives?— you may go to one station and he to the other of the telegraph cable which underlies that sea. "Tick, tick,"—the index registers something which shows that life, will — power, is at the other end. You cannot see your brother. No! He is thousands of miles away. You cannot hear him. No! That is of course impossible. But the "tick, tick" of the index,— you hear that; and in a minute the ticks have grouped themselves into a little foolish word, which was a bit of boyhood's nonsense between you and him, and which nobody on earth except you two understands. That is enough. You and he are together then, though ocean seem to part you. You make your signals, you send your token in reply, and the communion is established. Were you folded in each other's arms, kiss to cheek and breath with breath, it were not closer! Now, what shall you say? Shall you use this blessing only to go a begging? Shall you ask him to lend you a hundred dollars? Blasphemy! You will first say, "Is all well?" and he will say, "All's well," and you will say, "All's well." And then you will both pause; and if you have heart enough then to say the true thing, you will say, " So glad!" you will say, " Is not this too good?" "Is not this perfect?" For the mere sense and joy of reunion is more than enough to overwhelm every lesser thought or care or wish or anxiety.

From such an interview as that, the analogy holds right through to those interviews with God which we call our prayers. No man need try to tell beforehand what the token will be by which the present Father reveals himself to his eager child. But no man need try afterwards to prove to that child that he has received no answer and no token. The child knows too well. Again, no one need explain to the child that, as the world is ordered, he had better not ask for rain or for sunshine. The child did not seek his Father merely that he might be teasing him for presents. And, once more, the child will not be disconcerted because his prayer says so little,— because no words can tell his gratitude or his love; nay, because the words themselves provoke him, and stand in the way of his eagerness. Love always is greater and higher and nobler than the poor words which would express love. Yet, for all that, love does not refuse to use the words; nay, from every failure of the words true love rises with new determination that they shall express something, if not the whole. For love must speak, or it will die.

For ourselves, in our own prayer, the eternal lesson is that, for ourselves, we are to test the great experience of the noblest and best men and women of all ages. We are to try this great experiment of all. The finger-throb cannot be too light; the word cannot be too simple.

"Lord, I believe; help thou my unbelief."

Never was prayer more perfect.

"O my God, help me!"

No festival or fast, prolonged for weeks of ceremony, could say more.

"Come to me, O my Father."

This is to ask the whole.

After this manner, therefore, pray ye,—

"Our Father, who art in heaven."

RESPECTABILITY.

To be seen of men.— MATTHEW xxiii., 5.

I was present a little while ago in a company of thoughtful men, who happened to discuss the question of the place which respectability holds in one's religious or one's moral life. How far is it a religious advantage to be ranked among the "respectable classes"? or, how far is a man led into temptation by the mere fact that he is counted as a "respectable" man? How far do a man's own efforts falter, when he comes at that conclusion which St. Paul never came to,— the conclusion that he has attained, and is already perfect? There are some stiff things said in the Gospels about people in this condition: "Take heed to yourselves when all men speak well of you, for so did their fathers unto the false prophets." "There is more joy in heaven over one sinner that repenteth than over ninety and nine of you complacent people, who think yourselves so just that you need no repentance." Were these warnings temporary and local only, or do they belong to all time?

In the circle of gentlemen who discussed this, many of them leaders of thought, the question came up in this way: "A hundred and twenty years ago," it was said, "if a respectable man, who paid his debts punctually, was kind in his family, and obeyed the ten commandments, so far as was known,— if such a man chose to stay at home from religious service on Sunday, and in no way concerned himself with religious observance at home, the Christian ministers nearest him would make him and his the special subject of their prayer and effort. His life would be a rebuke to their apostleship. They would be sure he and his were going to hell, and they would be most eager to save him. But suppose such a man lives next door to your church now," it was said. "You do not think he is going to hell, and so you do not think it your business to save him. You may think his plan is a poor one, but you do not feel bound to interfere." And the inference was attempted, that in a higher regard for moral purity or moral obligation which our time expresses, there appears a less regard for religious sanctions, for religious observances, or, in one word, for religion.

I shall devote this morning to sorting out these questions with a view to answering them. Let me say, once for all, that there is danger in making too sharp a line between moral duties, as we call them, and what we call religious obligations. Let me say, once for all, that I know that much of the supposed difficulty which we consider, is a difficulty of language springing from looseness of language. People do not know what they mean when they say "religion," and they do not know what they mean when they say "morals." Bearing in mind this danger and trying to avoid it, I shall not attack the old disputed question, whether human righteousness is a "filthy rag" and how it is to be cleaned. But without that, we can consider the question, What are the dangers which environ us when all men think well of us?

I. But I am not going to entertain you with the old ascetic statement that a poor man is more sure of heaven than a rich man, or that our lives are more divine in proportion as we are uncomfortable. This is a very easy solution, and therefore a very frequent solution; but it is not a true solution. On the other hand, the coming in of God's kingdom, as I call it, the advance of civilization, as the newspapers call it, makes everybody richer; and it will continue to do so. The poorest beggar whom we relieve at the charity desk has some comforts that King Alfred did not have in his palace; nay, Queen Elizabeth in hers. It is no business of religion to diminish the comforts of life, or to diminish wealth. It is the business of religion to show men how to carry wealth and all the luxury that comes from it, "so that when these things fail," as they certainly will, "the angels of light may receive us into everlasting habitations." That is the Bible phrase, and we shall not improve upon it.

But is a man more sure of that harmony of life, that loyalty and strength which make up heaven in this world or another,— is he more sure of this when people think ill of him, when they scan him closely, when they inquire about his character, when they ask what letters of recommendation he brings, or who is his endorser? Is he more sure of a divine or godly life, of the kingdom of heaven St. Matthew would say,—than is that man whose business paper is rated as gilt-edged, whose social position is secure, who has never shocked society by the extravagance of his reforms, and who is supposed to do well and rightly the special duties which belong to his business? This is another question. And as most of us belong to these "respectable classes," this is a question for us to consider.

II. Here is the answer. Let other people think as well of us as they please, if we do not think too well of ourselves. The trouble with the Pharisees was not that they loved the praise of men. The praise of men is a perfectly legitimate praise when it is deserved and comes without seeking. The trouble was, that they loved the praise of men more than the praise of God. They came round to that point that, if they stood well up in the public opinion of Jerusalem, if they were in fashion, if they could command majorities, they were satisfied. They did not ask the other set of questions, whether they were carrying out God's plans, were working for him and with him, and whether, every day, they came nearer to him and nearer. Now here is a simple test of respectability, and one which any man, in his own case, can apply. Has he, in his pleasure that men think well of him, made the mistake of accepting their verdict instead of the verdict of his own conscience,—that inner verdict of the Divine Spirit which St. John defines, with perfect correctness, as the "praise of God"?

III. Now here I shall speak of the two dangers to a man who has achieved what I call "respectable position." The first is bred from one of the very qualities which is apt to secure that measure of success. It is the quality or habit of the man who takes care of his own concerns exclusively, and by no accident interests himself in those of other men.

" I care for nobody, no not I,
And nobody cares for me."

These are the words by which this habit is voiced in an old song.

Well, in speaking to men of affairs, as I am, I need not say that this habit, though unamiable, does go to what is called business success. The man who never goes to a party, who never takes his wife and children to a concert or a lecture, who sticks to his business so that he boasts to you that he has not left town in twenty years,— the man who, in this way, looks for what he calls the "main chance," is, in this abundant land of ours, tolerably sure to succeed pecuniarily. If, at the same time, he have the resolution to stick to one line of business and not to essay twenty, if he be not lured, as most New Englanders are of nature, to pass from one enterprise to another, such a man is quite sure, by the end of three and thirty years, to have amassed that amount of property which makes him, as far as means of that sort can make him, "respectable," in the parlance of the vulgar. But he has endangered himself all the while. He has been nursing that cursed falsehood which supposes he is a lonely atom in the world. He has, and this intentionally, cut off his ties with other men. Possibly he has not married. This would be the worst misfortune of all. Certainly, such a man as I have imagined,— I do not say that I ever saw such a man,— certainly he is not quick to see and to relieve the wants of those around him on any side of their lives. Even as to acquaintances, he only knows the men whom he has employed or has dealt with. As for friends, he cut himself off from the luxury of friendship the first time he truly sang,—

"I care for nobody."

Now friendship is the greatest luxury in life.

The danger in such a man's life is so clear that it does not take a moralist to point it out. Everybody sees it. The proverbs ridicule it. The popular stories of the world point scorn at it. The very word "miser," which once meant wretched or miserable, has come to mean this man who cares for nothing but the accumulation of money. And we need not look so far as the wretched miser of melodrama or the novel to see a kindred hardening of heart and narrowing of life in the man who can spend money, but can only spend it on himself, and who has not the habit of spending life, time, thought, sympathy, and love upon others. I know no more heart-rending story than a true story of one of the richest men this country has known, which points out the wretchedness I describe. Late one night he rang the door-bell of a neighbor, who hardly knew him by sight, so unsocial was he. With a blundering apology, he said he had come to ask this gentleman what would be a good public object for a man to spend his money on. And as the conversation went on, he broke into tears, I think, as he said, "Oh, my dear sir, if only my father had trained me to be looking out for those I could help, if he had early given me the pleasure of relieving the wretched!—instead of which I was taught to think for myself alone, and never by any chance to give away a penny for which I had no return."

When, in the discussion I spoke of, my friend said that in our day we did not think the Respectable Man he described was going to hell, and therefore we made no frantic efforts to save him, I said that it seemed to me many such men are in hell already, without knowing it. You know Swedenborg says that it is the worst of hell, that the damned are so low that they do not know what they have lost; they do not "think of the heaven which might have been theirs." What other name shall I give to the moral degradation, to the thick-skinned dulness, of the man who can only think of his own meals, and his own wines,—of his dividends and the other returns from his argosies; of the man who has no thought of his country's prosperity, no tear for the ravage of pestilence, so it is only far from his threshold, no thought for feeding the hungry, who have learned long since not to knock at his door, no help to the young aspirant who is doing his best, that the future may be better than the past? In the narrowness of such a life is a punishment self-wrought which language cannot describe. Nor is he the only sufferer.

It is not long since that I asked a teacher of large experience, who were the pupils whose chances seemed to be the worst. We had been speaking particularly of that pretence of indifference, the caring for nothing, good or bad, pretty or ugly, which is so sure to end in an insane asylum. My friend replied without a moment's hesitation. He even gave an instance, without a name. He said that, of all his pupils in that large and wealthy city where we then were, no one had so called out his whole sympathy and anxiety as a young girl left by the sudden death of her father the heiress of near a million dollars. And this was not, he said, the mere difficulty of wealth. My friend rated that low in comparison, and so do I. No! The trouble was, that the girl's father and mother had not been people who took a large view of life. They had lived for themselves rather than for mankind. And they had taught her to do so, by that silent example which is so effective. "I see no particular danger," said this teacher, "to boy or girl growing up in a rich family where people are doing their duty, where they maintain a large hospitality, where they are interested in the good causes which move the world, where life is made broad by the presence and sympathy of large men and large women, and many of them. The danger is where large ability has not created large sense of responsibility,— you have all this pressure from the weight of riches, and you have not created a strong character to bear it." There was the danger for the heiress for whom he feared. And he said — as he spoke with profound feeling — that what he feared for her was a narrow, small, prisoned, and caged-up life.

Such a prison as he feared for her, it happens that I remember. When I was two and twenty I happened to be in a distant city, where I met an old friend of my father. He had known of me from my birth. He asked me what my calling was to be, and I told him. "You are going to be a minister, are you?" he said,— with some doubt, I thought. "Well, now," he added, "do you know I think there are not many sinners among respectable people, among the people your father knows, among these people I know here? You'll not find many sinners. They are people who do about what is right, and they mean to. They are not people who commit sins." He meant to say that our profession was so far useless, if what we are for is "to save people from their sins." Some divine spirit guided my answer. I said, "Very likely it seems so. I suppose the sins of respectable people, such as you speak of, are generally their sins of omission, not their sins of commission." It was a most fortunate answer. He had not one word in reply. "Sins of omission," he said; "sins of omission,— yes, yes, sins of omission"; and then the conversation turned to other themes. Let me, in a few words, tell the close of his life. Many years after, I heard of him as retiring from business to enjoy his large fortune. Enjoy? What has a man to enjoy who, if he have committed few sins, has omitted the ministries and offices which unite a man to his race? Next, I began to hear of the habits of personal indulgence which come on a man who has not learned to live for mankind. And the last incident I ever knew of a life, which closed in utter darkness, was of his escape, naked, from his own house, of a winter night, in the madness of delirium tremens, pursued by the attendant whom for the moment he had deceived. Let a man care for himself, let a man worship himself, let him pamper his own comfort, feed his own palate, taste, hunger, thirst, and let him all the time be leaving out of thought the rest of the world in which he lives, and he is captive in the world of outer darkness, a world whose terrors cannot be exaggerated. Yes, and he is himself the judge who pronounces the sentence which consigns him to that world.

IV. I do not say, however, that a man saves himself from that outer darkness simply by trying to maintain his interest in other men. It is not so easy to do that. Men are not angels, and one may be discouraged. And the prosperous man, just in proportion as he is prosperous, must quicken the life which is the only life of any man, in securing his own intimacy, closer and closer every day, with a living God. Except the love of man and the sense of heaven,—and everything else grows weaker as a man grows older. But the knowledge of God, the thought of God,—nay, the very sight of God, for the pure in heart see God, and the love of God, for God's children do love him,—these grow as a man grows, and strengthen as his years increase. I may not be attracted by manly exercise as I was when I could walk thirty miles without fatigue. I may not care for reading as much as I did when I read a new novel every second day. Even the society of my neighbors may pall upon me because I have heard most of their reminiscences. And I may not enter upon politics quite so eagerly as did that young man who bore my name forty years ago, who was sure that only he could save the State. But, while these things fail me, the great reality does not fail. I live, and He whose son I am lives. He is—the Eternal—nearer me than any other friend, as his Life and Being are in and are beyond the farthest star. When I say this is right, it is he who prompts me. When I say I shall trample out that wrong, it is he who makes me almighty. Now, exactly the error and failure of these Pharisees, who held the high seats in the synagogues and loved the first places at feasts, was, that in that sort of life they had come to care for it more than they cared for God's praise and to come near to him. Well, this will happen when a man is looking for a comfortable house or for a good place in society, just as much as if he look for a good place at a Jews' feast or a high appointment at the synagogue. The cure for it is, that a man shall humbly seek God; that he seek him with that persistency that finds him; that he seek for him "with all his heart and all his soul." I do not say simply that he should go to church, though I do believe that so he answers one of the appeals which come to him in his very nature. No! I say that by all the ways by which he would seek the love of any other being whom he honored and revered he should seek to know God, to come near to him, and to love him. Yes, as a young lover recommends himself to her whom he would engage, by trying to do what she wishes, by carrying out, in new and original ways, designs she has formed, by reminding her of himself by whatever token of homage; as he recalls every word she ever said to him, and as he seeks every opportunity to speak to her,—so let a man seek after God, with all his soul and with all his strength. Let him find what God has for him to do, and do it. Let him find what God has said to him, and remember it. Let him speak to God to tell him what is on his heart, and let him listen to see what the Father has to say to his child.

Nor let any man fall into the natural mistake of saying "I will do this, but no man shall know I do it. This is a secret between God and me." There are those who have a share in such secrets. If you are seeking God's help for to-day's duty, these children around you have a right to know that you serve him and love him. Do not let them suppose that your own right arm or your own wit has achieved for you the comfort in which they live, or that you think so. Here is the blessing to them of any little office by which every day you and they join in worship. If you sing a hymn together, if you ask a blessing upon your food together, if you read to them a chapter in the Bible,—by whatever expression, though it be the simplest, show to your children, to your household, to your neighbors, what is your blood, whose child you are, and in whose service you belong. I say nothing here of what people call "professing religion." No gallant officer professes his courage. No great inventor goes round boasting of his skill. But every officer is proud of his uniform, which shows to whom he renders allegiance. And every great inventor would feel himself disgraced, if, in the simplest walk of his life, men could not trace the foresight and the precision by which he has compassed the victories which men owe to him. It is one thing to blow a trumpet in the synagogue. It is quite another, in the reverent and simple devotion of daily life, to say,—

"I also am a child of God."

V. Such duties may be summed up almost in a word. Let him who has achieved what the world calls success, let him whose position is endorsed as "respectable," take the gifts that God has given, as gifts given for a purpose. Do not let him boast that these things are his own. Let him hold them in trust for the common good. His pictures and statues, — let the world have the good of them. His library, his books, — let them be the common joy of his friends. His friends, — let him count among them the glazier that sets his window-glass; the gardener who brings to him his grapes; the boy who drives his Alderneys to pasture; and the fisherman who brings up his breakfast from the cove. His hospitality, — let it welcome this distinguished diplomat from England, that travelling princess from Russia, but let it welcome as well Bayard Taylor when he comes in the disguise of a travelling printer, or the milliner Phebe from Cenchrea, if she come that way on her modest business. This is it, — to keep open one's outlooks, and to claim the freedom of the world. Nor is it in this world only that my man of respectable position is to feel at home. He is to be a citizen of all worlds. He is to be able to take the wings of the morning, to ascend into the heights, to descend into the depths. His intercourse is not only with travellers or tradesmen, or with his children or his friends, — nay, it is not only with heroes, prophets, and poets of all past time. He is child of the Almighty, and with God himself he maintains his intimacy. Thus does he strike off and tread under foot the gyves and fetters of the world.

The next sermon of this series will be YOURSELVES, preached Jan. 12, 1879.

The sermons already published in this series are —

    THE GREAT HARVEST YEAR,
    LOOKING BACK,
    RITUAL,
    PRAYER.

They will be sent by mail, in answer to orders addressed to the Publishers, or to R. B. Palfrey, 12 Garland Street.

YOURSELVES.

Why even of yourselves judge ye not what is right?—LUKE xii.: 57.

The interesting and instructive address delivered at Birmingham by Dean Stanley, on his return from America, contains suggestions of the first value to us here; suggestions which it may be hoped will be remembered and considered. I say "hoped," for the observations of a visitor in such matters have much better chance for consideration than the same things when said by one of our own people. The stranger is not suspected of partisanship or personal prejudice. Thus, many a word of De Tocqueville is cited here as an axiom, which would have had no such weight were it quoted from Story or Kent or Webster. Of especial value to us is Dr. Stanley's instant observation, made with the promptness and decision of genius, that all the institutions of this country are at a different period of their crystallization from that in which the institutions of Europe are. He escapes entirely that preposterous "condescension of foreigners" which Mr. Lowell satirizes so happily. And he shames as well the ridiculous conceits of our own returning travellers, who would apply to a settlement on the prairie the police arrangements of Paris or of London. Dr. Stanley sees, from the very first, that the social institutions of America are as different from those of Europe as is her botany, or her geology, or her climate, or the system of the flow of her rivers, or the families of her native brutes. And, as a traveller in the West Indies is glad to find palm trees and canes instead of pines and blackberries, so Dr. Stanley has found one special enjoyment in his journey in noticing the essential differences between one civilization and another. He is not like my poor hero, of whom I think I have spoken here before, whose heart broke in a distant city because he found there on Sundays no "church of the second Presbyterian secession."

Now if any one of us here makes this observation, it seems as if he were shrinking from a difficulty. He feels himself, perhaps, like a scholar who says a word is not in the dictionary because he cannot find it there. It was two hundred years before our gardeners would accept the fact that our climate is different from that of Europe. Indeed, we generally imported the gardeners with their plants, and they tried to import the climate with them. French grape-vines, French clover, Spanish chestnuts, Scotch daisies, would be brought over and be put into the ground to perish, generation after generation, before people would accept the inevitable. Just in the same way you would find imported theologians, and imported politicians, and imported writers on social science bringing with them the systems they were used to, and insisting on their being tried here again. At this moment, I suppose, half the writers on the press of New York are men educated in English and Irish printing-offices; and it does not require a keen eye to trace in their articles the results of their education. So Mr. Agassiz once went to an office at Cambridge where they were printing a book of natural history for American schools. "Yes," said the great naturalist, "a book on butterflies for American school-boys; and there is not one butterfly represented that was ever seen alive in America." The printer had bought an invoice of cheap wood-cuts in England.

I am tempted, while this statement of Dr. Stanley's is fresh in your minds, to consider a subject which I might else have reserved for another occasion. But it is one which always engages the thoughts of observing men. It involves the duty presented in this text, a duty which in the peculiar circumstances of our crystallizing society comes in the very front of our social duties.

Here are these Pharisees, fixed in a mechanical etiquette, bound by a fashion two hundred years old, of trying to reproduce regulations made fourteen hundred years before.

Jesus Christ implores them to use their own sense of present duty. "Why even of yourselves judge ye not what is right?"

If he were speaking to us, he would use the same words, in addressing the grinding temptations of our own social system.

! To the citizen, ordered by a party organization to vote for men whose very existence he had never heard of before the ballot was put into his hands;—

"Why even of your own selves judge ye not what is right?"

To the woman in fashionable society, ordered to wear a costume which in another climate was invented by some disreputable person to call attention to her own vulgarity;—
"Why even of your own selves judge ye not what is right?"

To the teacher of children, asked to make the lively, electric young American work by the processes laid down for phlegmatic little Germans, born of other blood and trained under another sky;—
"Why even of yourselves judge ye not what is right?"

To the eager boy or the ambitious girl, reading in English novels of the adventures of dukes and duchesses, of the expenditure of millions for a *fête* and the waste of years in pleasure-hunting, or sighing when the mechanical tasks of a household call them back from such luxuries;—
"Why even of yourselves judge ye not what is right?"

And so in instances without end.

It has been again and again observed by the writers who study our institutions, that the danger of the American social systems is the loss of individuality. Mr. Stuart Mill was the first, I think, to suggest this danger, but a troop of English writers, including the novelists, follow him. We certainly see a marked difference ourselves between such men as Mr. Longfellow and President Pierce and Dr. Stowe, classmates though they were in the same college; and we can afford to laugh at the suggestion that our system makes all men into uniformed puppets. But none the less ought we to feel the tremendous might of social institutions like our own, and to guard against the pressure when manhood or womanhood is involved. Some wise American, I think Mr. Emerson, said that the test of a man here is whether there is grit enough in his make to defy even the millstone when it turns over him. For this pressure of society does become more and more powerful. When I was a boy, the head of a family directed the hours for the family breakfast. We boys had to adjust, as best we could, our own arrangements, and do as well as we could in making family arrangements and school arrangements accord. But I observe that in our time the school committee fixes the breakfast hour of every family in Boston. Meekly the heads of families conform to their requisitions. In the same way we all return from the country before summer is over,—at the direction of the school board; and we permit our children to study books which we should never ourselves have chosen, out of deference to what the majority has determined. It is in such loyalty to government that Mr. Mill and the rest find the danger that we shall lose our individuality.

Now the relief from such dangers is not the tame expedient of removing the pressure. It is the brave determination to increase the strength which sustains it. When an Attila threatens the Roman Empire, we must not buy off Attila; we must strengthen the Roman fortresses and armies. We want a strong State. We want schools, railways, societies, and other orders of service large enough and strong enough for anybody. And because of this we must have strong men and women; men and women who assert their own individual life with such energy and heart that the social life shall not tyrannize. Because the sun's attraction draws the planet so strongly, the planet must move all the more resolutely in its own orbit, that it shall not be absorbed and devoured by the sun. Man *is* a member of society. And society *is* very strong. But, all the same, man is a separate child of God, and from that Almighty God man inherits his nature; nay, of that Almightiness man partakes, when he will. It is therefore to man as child of God that the great word comes, "Why even of yourselves judge ye not what is right?" And it is for every man of us eagerly to consider what is the personal addition he must make to the work of the social system in which he lives.

I am tempted by Dr. Stanley's remark to take an illustration from certain duties which seem almost feudal, though they belong to the system — not in the least feudal — in which we live. We are much nearer to the duties of a simple social order than they are in England. Indeed, half the follies of our young people of all classes come from the English stories which they read, and from an unconscious effort to introduce customs which are really as foreign to us as were Mr. Agassiz's butterflies. It was in this way that in my own time, we have been fairly laughed out of the use of that good word "help," which indicated very precisely what was a reality in our social order. We were compelled to substitute the word "servant," for which we had no precise analogue. Now the truth is that the New England farmer or manufacturer or housekeeper, who will remember that the people whom he employs help him and help him very materially, and that there is a correlative obligation that he shall help them, shows he understands the real social order of New England.

He leaves that social order for another if he imitate old Wade Hampton of South Carolina, who knew his own people so little that he asked one of his own slaves in the street who his master was. The slave did not know his master, and the master didn't know his man. It is not long since, that one of our large manufacturers here took a class of grown-up boys in a mission Sunday-school. More and more interested in them, he asked about their daily lives,— " For whom do you work, and you, and you?" When he came to the third, the boy said simply, "I work for you, sir," without any sense of humor or complaint. But the gentleman to whom he spoke, to whom I owe the story, took the lesson home. It quickened him to new effort in just such work as he was then engaged in, that he might not be shamed again in failing to recognize one of those who was loyally working for his interests. Whatever be the method by which the master of workmen can assert his individuality in the midst of the stress and pressure of the great machine to which they all belong,— his constant assertion of that individuality will prove to be so much gain. Let him show his personal interest in them and theirs outside the mere mechanical interest, which unites them only as the wheels of a steam-engine are united. In such case you judge for yourself what is right, and are more than the slave of a Sanhedrin or a trades-union.

I have alluded to the pressure of the public system of education. Its stress is sometimes ludicrous. I knew a boy who was studying his geography lesson for school, — on a visit at his uncle's house. The school maps were so bad as to try his eyes severely, and his aunt substituted much better maps from one of the renowned printing-offices of Belgium. But, after a little, the honest boy brought back the good maps and said, "I ought not to use these, because they give me such an advantage over the other boys in the class who have not this atlas." Nor is this a mere freak of conscience of a sensitive boy. I am afraid the masters of his school would confirm his decision, and very likely the school committee would confirm them. That is to say, they would think it decidedly better to have this boy learn his lesson badly; in order to keep the regiment in step, all of whom were learning their lessons on bad maps. And so the original object, which is that the boy shall learn something useful, is wholly lost sight of, that the minor advantage may be gained, and the discipline of the school not interfered with. All this is wrong, and we should set our faces against it at every point.

We should make study as agreeable to the children as we can, — as little formal, and as much a part of life as possible. As things stand, the presence in a French class of a boy who has lived in Paris a year and can speak French is counted disastrous. Nobody knows what marks to give him, or how to discount what is regarded as his unfair advantage. An ingenious teacher will even set him to studying Choctaw while the others write their French exercises. But in truth there is no more inequality between him and the rest, than between a boy born shy and one who is ready, or between one who is born with a good verbal memory and one who has none.

If any prophet could succeed in teaching the lesson of individual duty in the matter of charity relief, all that business would fairly adjust itself, and our elaborate organizations would tumble to pieces because they would have nothing to do. This renowned Elberfeldt system, of which we hear a good deal, and of which I hope we shall hear more and more, amounts to this: that no visitor to the poor has more than three or four families in charge. But better yet is the individual system. If every family in Boston which has means enough made itself — yes — intimate in some one of these families which need the help of what we call outside relief, all our formal "visitings" would be unnecessary, all danger of creating a pauper class would be ended, and all the friction and screaming of our poor-law machinery would come to an end. Yes, and more than that: we should put the round peg in the round hole and the square peg in the square hole. We should not have a lad put into the place of a cash boy who ought to be apprenticed to a machinist. We should not make a bungling machinist of the boy who ought to begin by being a cash boy. We should send the young Robinson Crusoes to sea. And we should send to the West the other boys who are born with a divine instinct for the farm. All such detail of success is due to personal interest, — nay, to personal attention and affection; and such victories come in proportion as we are not satisfied with twenty annual subscriptions to twenty organized charities, but as every man selects for himself some one thing which shall be done well. "Why not of thine own self judge thou what is right?"

I might sum up all these separate suggestions by the single observation, — which for myself and my children I always try to keep in mind, — that there are very few of us here who, in the line of one or another ancestor, are more than three or four generations from a log cabin. And such is the glad freshness of our life that there is not one of these boys or girls who hear me but may indulge the hope of living in a log cabin, or in something akin to it, before he dies, or she. It is all very fine to read of Lothair leading Corisanda through files of servants in livery, to dine from gold plate as a band of music plays airs from Schubert. But Mr. Disraeli himself writes this as burlesque; and for us, — we are neither Lothair nor Corisanda. We are decent people, of average intelligence, who have to earn our own livings, whose fathers blacked their own shoes and whose mothers kneaded their own bread. Let us see that our sons know how to black their own shoes well, and that our daughters can make as good bread as our mothers could. I do not say that they must do it every day. I do say that they should know how to do it. Cœur de Lion himself could not have been dubbed and belted as a knight unless it were sure that he could shoe his horse, saddle him and bridle him, bleed him if he needed bleeding, groom him when he needed grooming. It might not come to Cœur de Lion, King of England, to do this once in ten years. But he must not order others to do it unless he could do it himself. That is the reason why I ventured to use the word "feudal" in the midst of customs which had not a feudal origin. It is not the habit of our own people to lose sight of such necessities. The education at West Point is a fair type of the common-sense requisitions of the country. You owe it to that education that there is not a major-general in your army who is not perfect in the school of the soldier. Nay, if need be, he can cut cartridge paper and make a cartridge. If need be, he can thread his needle and make a sand-bag for an embrasure. If need be, he can mix the chemical salts which shall ignite a shell. If need be, he can make the electric battery which shall explode a shell. There is the true system of American life. When we carry it out as we ought we shall be spared the hardships which European emigrants expose us to. It was a set of foreign principles and foreign habits which made the strikes which blocked your Pennsylvania railways two years ago. For a strike is wholly un-American. And how had you prepared to meet one? Who were your officers in charge? Had they been trained in every early step of their profession? Did they know how to build an engine, how to fire it, and how to run it? Or had they been selected, as if they were Englishmen, because they were the nephews of uncles, — because they were young gentlemen of family, who wanted good positions? You would not fear a strike of railroad engine-men if, from the president of your road down to the ticket-sellers, every officer in your staff knew how to run an engine. When Murat, King of Naples, is known to be the best horseman in the cavalry of Napoleon, there is not a soldier in the cavalry but is proud to follow where Murat leads the way. And, by precisely that rule — by precisely the respect with which men follow the leaders whom they know to be leaders — are you to repress disorder, and regulate all those ebullitions of temper which never rise unless men suspect that those who are called their leaders are not fit to lead.

"Why even of yourselves judge ye not what is right?" What I am now to say may be said in few words, because I speak of the simplest field for such independence; but its importance is infinite. In your prayer, in all your worship, in all the relations of religion and religious service, why even of yourselves judge ye not what is right? It is nothing to you that some fool has said in his heart that there is no God. It is for you to try the experiment, to come to God day and night in your prayer, and see if abundant life do not enliven you, as is promised. It is nothing to you that this preacher or that has wrought out some cruel notion of God from this prophecy or that epistle. It is for you to judge what is right and true, from a conscience as quick as his, from your own experience of life, and from your own test of the love that shows itself in all the world. And it is nothing to you that a hierarchy of priests, owing their appointment to others like themselves, in the narrowness of a close corporation, lay down this condition or that of confession or of ritual for you. Why not of yourselves judge what is right, and come to your Father as you would have your children come to you, frankly, gladly, and without any interpreter? Here is the freshness of the walk with God. Here is the sincerity of worship uncontrived. Here is the enlargement of life which comes to those who see God with no screen between. They receive life directly from Him whose sons they are.

7

WHAT IT IS TO BE CATHOLIC.

Go ye into all the world, and preach the gospel to every creature. — MARK xvi., 15.

The discussion of ritual, on which I ventured on the anniversary of this church, is not complete, if we confine our notion of the ritual of religion simply to church observances. A certain looseness of thought in this matter gives rise to doubts and other difficulties. Thus does it happen that young travellers in other lands contrast the simplicity of American ritual with the grandeur of religious service which they see in Europe, and that the contrast is to the disadvantage of home.

Their notion about the contrast is just the same — if they would analyze it — as is men's notion of all the other contrasts between our life and that of Europe, — contrasts which Dr. Stanley stated so fitly in that address to which I referred the other day. Thus there is hardly an entertainment offered to a traveller in Europe more attractive than one of the great military reviews of St. Petersburg or of Paris. There are some of us who have seen at home, alas! reviews of more men, and men who had had more experience in arms. But in general, thank God! the young American of to-day has never seen a thousand men drawn up in array for battle. There is many an American boy or girl who has never seen a professional soldier in his life. To the traveller from another continent, almost the first question here is, "Where are the soldiers?" And the amused answer of his American host is, "Where should there be any soldiers? Certainly not in a peaceful town." What happens, of course, then, is that the young American traveller is interested, as no Frenchman or Russian can be, in a great review. And when he sees that magnificent pageant, the precision of movement, the evident power of massing great bodies of men for a certain specified purpose, he may well be delighted, if he be surprised. But, if he be a very young observer, and if he know very little of history, he may ask, "What would come to my country, if she were in collision with this country? Where should we be, if the force of these legions were turned against us?" If he be very young and very timid, he will ask if America ought not to be on the alert in providing for herself such an army. Now this experience, perfectly natural, about a highly organized army is repeating itself all the time about a highly organized church. There is much instruction to one who will watch the process by which so many clergymen of the English Establishment have been lured into the service of the Roman Church. Belonging to a school which believed in orders of service, in diligent training and close discipline, they said — not unnaturally — at last, "We will go where they have most experience in this thing,— where they have done it longest and do it best." It is precisely as in 1815, at the end of our short war with England, young American gentlemen who had made an essay in arms here crossed the ocean as soon as Napoleon landed from Elba, to seek service under him. If a man is interested in a method or organization, he likes to go where that method is best pursued.

Standing aloof from both sides, we see very distinctly that this process goes on, and is not unnatural. But perhaps we do not see that it is the same process at bottom, where one of our own young people is involved. I remember a companion of my own in college, brought up under the religious administration of one of our Boston Unitarian churches, with very little of form, and a careful concealment of such organized activity as it had. This young gentleman came to Rome in his travels. At Rome he made the acquaintance, somewhat intimate, of a Jesuit priest, — an accomplished man, not much older than himself. It was not long before he became the companion of this gentleman and his friends. Soon he was glad to render this or that service which a layman could render. All the time he was watching the efficient machinery which the Roman Church has at work at Rome for the carrying forward its purpose. At that time its staff in the city of Rome was so large that every eighth man in that city was a priest, in one or another grade of service. By precisely the instinct which I have described in the matter of arms and armies, — the instinct by which a young man of spirit goes where men do best the thing he likes to see done,— my young friend, a man of courage and unselfish life, became so much interested in what he saw of the effective work of the Jesuit order that he united with it, and in its service, or slavery, he died.

Now I think that that is as bad a thing as can happen to a man. The moment when a man signs his own death warrant, when he says, "I resolve that I will never make another resolution," seems to me the saddest crisis of the saddest tragedy. "I can think now, and what I think is that I will never think any more." So is it that the poor wretch ties a cannon-shot to his feet, and then rolls himself from the deck into the sea! It is awful to imagine. Yet I think that I know perfectly well how this brilliant and loyal fellow came to this pass. I think he had gone to Europe — as so many other Americans have gone — with no knowledge of what we have at home. Just as you shall see travellers enjoying the prettiness of the Staubach who have never been awed before the marvel of Niagara, so you see such young Americans delighted with the organization of Rome who know nothing of what Jesus Christ and the religion called by his name have worked at home, and are still working here.

The analogy with military organization holds completely. It is only the young American, and he who is very ignorant of history, who is deceived by the brilliancy of uniform, the facility of concentration, and the skill in tactics, so that he supposes that Russia or France is the strongest power in the world. The American who is older, and who knows more of history, remembers how, at the call of his country, millions of men sprang to arms,— sailors for the navy, landsmen for the army. He remembers the marvels of engineering, of sanitary care, of organization in all its forms, which the good-sense of an excited country brought into every department of the system and discipline of arms, — marvels which the general staffs of Europe have been glad enough ever since to study. He remembers marches of which no military history has the precedent, battles with whose severity no modern battles can compare, and an army which disbanded itself as easily as it formed itself, — which when it disbanded itself was the most formidable army which the nineteenth century had seen. Remembering this, he is amused indeed, nay he is instructed, as he looks on what is called a field-day in a review at Paris, or at St. Petersburg; but he does not so much as ask the question whether his own country needs any such arrangements as these at home.

In precisely the same way, the American who has a fair

idea of his country's history, who knows that our social
order, more than that of any people, has been controlled by
Christianity,— nay, is to this hour,— is amused by the great
ecclesiastical organizations of Europe, but not tempted to
follow them. We have washed our hands of the old mechanical alliance of the Church and the State. With our eyes
open, we have adopted the wiser principle by which the spirit
which inspires the Church shall be made to quicken the legislation of the State, and to enliven every State undertaking.
The American, even of average intelligence, ought to see
this, and to see why we are not to transfer to such a land
even the most successful ecclesiastical arrangements of another.

I may fairly tell an anecdote of an enthusiastic young
friend of mine, who had an occasion to visit a Roman Catholic bishop; for he was himself as ready as any one, afterwards, to laugh at his own enthusiasm. " It was delightful,"
he said. "It was just like a book. In the porch of the
bishop's house were old-fashioned benches at the right and
left, and there sat these dear old beggars, waiting to be cared
for. And then a man came out and gave to one a pair of
shoes, and to another a loaf of bread, and to another a pair of
mittens. Was it not perfectly lovely? So like what a bishop
should be?" I was a little older and less credulous. I had
some experience of being a bishop myself, in a small way.
I said I should like it better if these aged people had been
seen to in their homes by a more modest ministry. I said
the business of the Church was so to quicken the charities
of the State that this wholesale alms-giving, the parent of
laziness and beggary, should be impossible. I remembered
very well that Cardinal Wiseman justified the beggary every-
where patent in the city of Rome, on the principle that the
Roman Church wishes to remind every passer-by of the suf-
ferings of a common humanity. Protestants, he said, shut
up the sick in infirmaries. Rome reminds the well of their
pain, by letting them beg in the streets for their relief. Now
of that system the test is the Golden Rule. If Cardinal
Wiseman were aged, lame, and blind, would he prefer to be a
beggar in the street, rain and shine, summer and winter, or
would he prefer to be in the comfortable parlor of an Old
Man's Home? If we are Christians, we must do as we would
be done by. And in this specific business of the relief of the
poor, the Church attained its greatest triumphs when it
drove Protestant England and Protestant America up to the

position which Catholic Spain and Catholic France never dared to take. That position is that the town where a man is born, or where he has acquired his settlement, is, to the last, responsible for his care. Is he blind, the whole neighborhood must support him. Is he insane, the whole neighborhood must care for him, and that with the most exquisite relief. Is he hungry, the neighborhood must feed him, and that with no faltering or spasmodic ration, but with the regularity that gives to him each day his daily bread. So long as the systematic care of the poor is assumed by Protestant States, and is not assumed by Catholic States, so long will the Protestant Church have the right to say that it has succeeded in a branch of Christian effort where the Roman system has failed. And this, indeed, is conceded by at least one Catholic writer, who has studied that matter profoundly.*

Till the community has spent its last crumb, every man shall be fed who needs. Every man. That truly catholic answer made the poor-laws of England and New England. No Roman Catholic jurisprudence has ever yet made that answer. The convents may be liberal. But how if their supply comes to an end? The churches may be liberal. But they can give no more than they have. And to convent or to church a man must appeal for a favor, and not claim the right of a child of God. The poor-law of England and of New England — ridiculed and abused though it often is — rests on a deeper foundation, and on the only true one. It rests on this foundation: that every man has a right to his life. Come pestilence, come famine, come internal convulsion destroying trade, — a Christian State owns under this law that it must feed every man, woman, and child. They do not sue for this as beggars. The law gives it to them as their own. And to give it to them every penny in the land is pledged, if need be, that the naked and hungry shall be clothed and fed. The supply does not cease till the richest prince in the land is at his last crust. The law shares that crust with all.

I speak in this detail, because, once for all, the Christian care of the poor by the State illustrates the whole Puritan system. The same contrast between the Puritan system and the Roman system appears in the care of the sick, in the

* Lamartine, who ought to know, — and who says that France would have been saved every lawless outbreak of half a century had France risen to the level of the principle of the poor-law of Elizabeth.

methods of education, and in every other detail. The effort of the Roman system is to do all that is possible by the hands of ecclesiastics. The great success of the Puritan system is to need as few ecclesiastics as possible, in bringing the officers of the State up to carry forward for every one the duty which the conscience of the Church sees should be done. The results are magnificent. They are more than princely. In education, for instance, the Roman Church says, "See how democratic is our priesthood. Here is the child of a peasant, and he began by being a choir-boy in the church; but he was watched and cared for and educated, and to-day he is a bishop,—nay, perhaps a pope." But a Puritan State would say, "That is nothing in comparison with our applied Christianity. You educate such priests as you need. Where is your training of the rest? Where is your training of woman, for instance? We offer the same privilege to every child of God. Nor is there anything but his own refusal to bar the foundling in the gutter from a competition for the highest honors of the university."

Such boasts are repeated, I know, only too often in the Messages of our Presidents and the orations of the Fourth of July. I have no occasion to repeat them as matters of boast, excepting so far as I place the credit of such achievements where it belongs, with the Christianity of America, and the origin of it with the Puritan Christianity of America. And my special wish is to connect the contrast we have been tracing with the study of the rituals of churches,—with their methods of worship. If the Roman Catholic Church elects to carry on by its priesthood all these varied offices, it will have a very large priesthood, and it will have all the elaborated formality which to a large priesthood belongs. When the Puritan church determined to trust to its laity nine out of ten of these duties, it virtually abandoned that elaborate formality which to the Roman Church gives its charm. Grant that the fathers of New England built ugly meeting-houses instead of stately churches. Grant that they droned through prosy hymns where others sang stately ancient chorals. Still the men who, as a part of their service of God, taught any beggar's brat to read the Scripture in the original, and to any beggar's brat offered in all distress the last crumb for comfort and the last drop for cure, certainly contrived the ritual which best meets all divine requisition. What doth the Lord require of thee but to do justly, to love mercy, and to walk humbly with thy God?

And the lesson which I am urging on my young friends is involved in this statement. When your time comes to travel, you go to the Convent of the Gray Nuns in Montreal to see their care of the orphans, and to the Black Nuns to see their care of the aged. In Paris, you see a sister of charity take care of a *crêche*, and when you come to Rome your guide takes you to the College of the Propaganda. You are present at an exhibition where pupils from fifty lands speak, each in his own tongue, the marvellous works of God in a display surpassing the marvel of Pentecost. In the Sistine Chapel, the chosen choir of the world sings the Ave Maria or the Miserere as angels might sing it. And you are so fortunate as to listen to the strain, and I hope to join in the devotion. How matchless the display! Yes! But display is not the only object of religious ritual. Before you ask yourself that uneasy question, "Why is all this forbidden to a Protestant?" ask yourself one or two questions as to what Puritan ritual would have to show to a Roman visitor. Ask yourself first of all how far you are fit to be his guide, if he should come to visit the city which the Puritans left as the monument of their victories.

"Black nuns, gray nuns, sisters of charity, sisters of mercy, sisters of the bleeding heart," — you have made yourself familiar with the long catalogue in your travels : how much do you know of the enginery by which the same work is better done in your own home? How many of the schools have you ever seen which one sister of your own here has established for the very poorest children of Boston? How far are you acquainted with the detail of the charity work of that bureau of charities which is studied by every intelligent traveller from every nation in the world? Did you ever make the little voyage to the island yonder which should enable you to say how far the Christianity of this town cares for its aged? Have you ever entered the hospital yonder which shows how far the Christianity of this town cares for the sick who are in need? Some of you live in Roxbury. Did you ever take a book or a battledore or a shuttlecock to the hundred and more orphan boys whom a Christian city trains there for manly life? More than this : in the order of a Puritan church you are ordained and crowned, you are priest and king, to take your part in these offices. It may be a very humble part; it may be to take a cripple to ride; it may be to amuse a sick child in a hospital. But the theory — the magnificent theory of the Protestant Church — is that you also have your own turtle-dove to bring to God, and that no priest nor mitre nor tiara may stand between.

It is in the administration of religion for everybody that the Church attains its proud title — Universal. *Universal:* a church for rich and poor, prince and peasant, beggar and nabob, black, white, and red. Universal: a church for wise and unwise, people of culture and people of none. Its charities, its education, its hospitality, its worship, must be universal. This great word universal, in the Greek language, is "Catholic," and to this great claim the Greek Church and the Roman Church aspire. But neither of them has proved its claim, and neither of them has deserved it. So the name "Catholic," with its great meaning forgotten, is now the name of a large schismatic sect, which is the most divided and separated from the Church Universal of them all.

What is to come, as the centuries pass, from the cradle of Bethlehem and from the cross of Calvary, is a united world,— one body of many members, all caring for each, and each for all. Rightly and naturally the Church, even in the swaddling clothes of its infancy, in which it is still stumbling and halting, keeps this end in sight, and strives to maintain the semblance of it, if nothing more. To be a universal church is a necessity for it. It is nothing if not universal, — if its arrangements of ritual and teaching, if its doctrine and its history, cannot be adapted to black, white, and red, to learned and unlearned, old and young, rich and poor.

Our duty is, and our joy, so to administer religion that it shall not be a luxury for the rich, not a secret for the learned, not a talisman for those initiated, but that it shall be light and life for all. And this is no matter of the service of this house alone. It is in your daily welcome to those whom you meet more than half way, it is in your daily tenderness to those whom you employ, as you show the spirit of Christ to this stranger, to that stupid companion, to this man unfortunate in his ventures, to that woman unamiable and alone,— that you bring in the kingdom. Your church becomes the holy catholic church, if your administration of religion is like your Father's who is in heaven.

He maketh his sun to rise on the evil and on the good, ar sendeth rain on the just and on the unjust.

THE JOY OF LIFE.

The law of the spirit of life hath made me free.—ROMANS viii., 2.

In one of his early novels, Mr. Disraeli makes his hero say that he enjoyed living for itself. It was a pleasure to him to live; he knew it was, and he enjoyed it without seeking more perhaps. Least of all did he try to prove to himself why he enjoyed it, as if it were a strange thing that life itself should be joy.

He often repeats the remark in those novels, which are among the more remarkable philosophical works of our time. It probably contains the secret of a certain elasticity in his own life,—unwillingness to brood over failure, and certainty of success,—which encourages all his followers, drives his enemies almost to distraction, and, indeed, has given to him the popular reputation which is quite inadequate, though it be so natural, of being not so much a far-sighted statesman, carrying out through life one fixed plan, but rather a pet child of fortune, who always lights upon something bright and happy. It is not in Mr. Disraeli's immediate purpose to impress the profound religious significance of his remark. Yet, while it traverses squarely all Calvinism and most of the theories of the Roman Catholic Church, it embodies the profoundest spirit of pure Christianity. It is well enough announced in the familiar story of the cheerful old lady who rebuked some book-made advisers, when they came to her to instruct her on her relations to God. "Do you not think it very strange," they whined, "that this great God, this Infinite Being who rules all worlds, can stop to think of a worm like you, and care for your happiness and comfort in a thousand ways, some of them so small and delicate?"

"I do not think it strange at all," said the old saint. "I think it is just like him."

It is sad, however, that in Christian lands, among Christian people, there should be any question as to the religious side of the duty which bids us make the most good we can out of life. It is sad enough that a Church founded by a Leader who said, first, last, and always, that "the kingdom of heaven is at hand," should so sedulously teach that the kingdom of heaven is not now or here, but in the future and in another place. The result of this is, that the great body of Christians really think they please God here merely by doing what is disagreeable. If they wear clothes they do not like, if they eat food that is unpalatable, if they spend time in reading dull books,— such people think that there is an element of virtue in the fact that the thing done is not joyous. It is sad, again, that when Jesus Christ sedulously told all men to become "as little children," wishing them to take life with the heartiness and straightforward simplicity with which children take it, his Church should as sedulously try to interest children in cares and anxieties which at the worst belong only to mature age. To tried and anxious men and women Jesus Christ says, "Become as little children." But his Church is too apt to say to joyous boys and girls, "Become ye as like as you can to little old men and women."

I. Now here is the central truth: This Infinite Holy Spirit, who is present with us, whose name is God, who smiles in the sunbeam and breathes in the zephyr, is light, and knows no darkness at all. That is St. John's grand phrase. "God is love," is another such sweeping statement. He *lives*, and whoever lives in him cannot die. That is, in substance, Jesus Christ's phrase. Human expressions which make separate parts of this same statement are, that God enjoys his own work; that whatever he does is good.

Now mankind, men and women, you and I for instance, are his children. By this phrase, which is hardly metaphorical, is meant that we inherit his nature; our lives are from his life; our thoughts are from his thought; our joys are from his joy. What he purposes for the world we can purpose, and in part perform. And when he makes the world so that it is in harmony with his own being, so that, as all the poets tell us, all Nature is a visible type of his invisible spirit,— why, this same world is therefore in harmony with our being also, and Nature is something which we need not only study from without as observers, but of which we can apprehend the life and enter happily into the plan. No! I did not make the stars and arrange them in the constellations. I did not draw the black curtain of the night and scatter them over it in numbers beyond number, to make it glorious.

I have never taught that night to grow gray and pale and at last golden, and then to blush with hope and joy. I have never sent the sun careering through it, to "rob their radiance from the stars," and to make the whole earth laugh with beauty and joy. But I am the child of the God who did this. As Moses put it, I am "made in his image." As St. James put it, I am "partaker of his nature." As Jesus Christ put it best of all, I am his son, and his beloved son at that. And it is simply for me "to assert my birthright," as we say so often. It is simply for me to be what I am. It is for me to act as a child in his father's home, who knows that he belongs there; knows who he is, and for whom these treasures and comforts, these luxuries and joys, were collected. When I forget the past, am not anxious about the future, but live the life of to-day, do the duty of to-day and enjoy the joy of to-day, I live as a child of God. When I feel what Jesus Christ said, "Sufficient unto the day is the evil thereof," I gratefully accept God's blessings for to-day, as little anxious about to-morrow, indeed, as is the lily when it throws open its glories to the sun.

II. The illustrations which I have thus used come, by a simple enough law, from the use of what we choose to call physical Nature. And those illustrations imply what is perfectly true, that if we would study external nature more, if we would look more with our eyes, listen more with our ears, — nay, if we would know more about nature, or take more interest in the world in which we live,— we should be, I need not say happier, but better, men and women. Happiness, it is true, is a matter not to be studied for or prearranged. But goodness, which means at bottom unity with God,— that can be sought; and he who seeks for it with all his heart will find it. Now the matter of an interest in the visible world is one where we who live in cities are apt to be in danger; most of all, those of us who are born in cities. It is so convenient to have your boy and girl in the house, that the boy who stays in-doors poring over books comes in the way of being called, for that mere habit. "a good boy." Perhaps he is a good boy, and perhaps the books are good for him. But perhaps, again, they are bad for him; and the danger comes in, that he will be losing the habit of quick observation of what God has made. The old story of "eyes and no eyes" is apt to illustrate the difference between the boy trained in the country, with his eyes open to every trace, like an Indian's, and the boy trained in the city, who does not know a rabbit's hole when he sees it. To form the habit of watching the work of Nature, is to take a step in moral training as well as in mere information. And here I am not satisfied with that somewhat purblind study which is called the study of natural history in most schools. I am pleading not so much for the classification of plants or animals as I am for keen and sympathetic observation of all the works of God around us. To know the shapes of the flakes of snow; to make acquaintance with the lichens on the sticks of wood in the wood-pile ; to stand by when the fishermen yonder on the pier unload their captures early in the morning, and to know their prey ; to follow the movement of the stars month by month ; to catch the most infrequent planet, and be ready for the rare conjunction,— such are bits of personal training as possible for him who lives in a crowded street in Boston as for him who is in the most lovely country town. And so, the moment when spring releases us, to know where the earliest maple blossom and saxifrage can be found within a ten-miles' walk of Boston,— he who trains himself to such pleasures may have the kingdom of his heaven indeed at hand.

I might fairly make the comparison here which I made the other day, when I compared the activity of travellers with the sluggishness of us who stay at home. My young friends will hurry from England to Norway to overtake the June steamer up the coast, so that at midnight, beyond the North Cape, they may see the Midnight Sun ; or they will ascend the Righi at night, and spend the night there that they may have the chance to see the sun rise from the mountain-top. "If the prophet bid them do some great thing, would they not have done it?" But let it be a little thing,— let it be to see the glory of sunrise from the top of the Blue Hills, or from the end of Long Wharf,— nay, from the top of the house in which we sleep,— and how many of us hug the pillow yet again ! So hard is it to remember that heaven is around us always, and that the greatest marvels are at hand. The growth of an elm tree is as wonderful as that of a palm. The crystallization of an icicle is as exquisite as that of a diamond. But it is this people whose heart is waxed gross, who have eyes but they see not, and ears but they hear not; and this is the reason they do not understand.

III. For it is the same set of habits, the rather pressing routine of crowded life, which closes our ears so that we do not hear. For this we have, in cities, our advantages, which should be our compensation for the loss of those sights of outward Nature which, of our free will, we have destroyed. We are surrounded by men and women worth hearing. Well for those who use their opportunities. But if you will let me speak of myself, I remember with shame that while I grew to the age of twenty in this town, through the very years in which Channing made his fame, I never heard him preach. "I could do it any time," I said. So I never did it. The first prophet of my time, here he was proclaiming the gospel on which turns the salvation of this century from cant and form. I was myself under his power, made by what he was saying, and yet I never saw him in the pulpit, nor heard him speak there. I had the honor of knowing him,—of intimacy in his house. He was kind to me as he was to all children; but such is this power of routine, that I, who of course always meant to listen to his preaching, never did. Do not be guilty of such folly. Whenever any prophet rises, whether in religion, in politics, in art, in literature, whoever he be or whatever he say,—whenever you have a chance to see and hear an inspired man, use it for your blessing. Here is the reason why we are always telling young people to find, once a day, some one whom they know to be their superior. It may be an actor on the stage, a blacksmith at his forge, a pure, sweet saint looking death in the face in his bedroom, an active man of affairs, a traveller of wide experience. I care not what the form which life takes in its exhibition. Sun yourself in that life, so that you may not be satisfied with your own littleness. "He that has ears to hear let him hear."

IV. All such habits go to what Lord Houghton calls, so well, the joy of eventful living. That joy is within the hand of any one who will clutch for it; but no man can have it who does not seek. It is not the special joy of kings or officers of State. It is in the power as well of the gamin of the street, if he know how to seek for it. I need not take a costly ticket to the opera in my search for it. The boy who stands before Punch and Judy on the Common takes more genuine delight than the critic in his stall, because the boy is willing to be delighted. Let a man remember, whatever his position, that it is of him, and others like him, that history is made; and let him be sure that, whatever his ignorance of past history, he assert his place as a part of the history of to-day,—at least that he hold a lamp well filled as the chariot of its triumph goes by. I remember how, in the war, I chafed because our brave boys were going off from the church here, month by month, to battle, while I was left at home to send lint and ether after them. I could not satisfy myself till I, too, had seen an army, and ridden as near to Richmond as a loyal man could go. But that sort of eagerness ought to fill up life in ways different from travel. In those same war days we all hung with amazement on the tale of the Monitor as she fought the Merrimac; of the Nahant when she took the Atlanta. We read the description of our little champions in the newspapers, and because an American invented the Monitor each one of us was proud he was an American. Yes; and it was a walk of perhaps two miles from this place to the yard where that little Nahant was built, under the direction of one of our own number here. I do not suppose ten people of this congregation had the curiosity to see what was, at the moment, one of the wonders of the world. Had we visited New York we should have looked for it. But here at home the routine of home was too much for us. Nor need I speak of such exceptional inventions. How universal the remark that it is not till some friend visits us, from Europe or from the South or West, till we have to show the wonders of a favored city, that we begin to know what these wonders are.

Now such failures do not spring, I think, from accidental temptation of fashion, or of other routine. They come from the failure to regard life itself as the blessing of blessings. He who squarely determines to live while he lives, to use his life to-day and not to put off till to-morrow the use of it,— this man knows what man is doing to-day, and knows what God is doing. This man enjoys the changes of nature, and lives in the changes of history. He wins "the joy of eventful living," because he lives the infinite life,— the life of an immortal. This man takes in the sense of Him who came to give us life more abundantly.

V. See how his habit applies in the company he keeps. He is not confined to that ghastly little *coterie* of the people who live in the same street, or that other *coterie*, not less ghastly, of those whose clothes are made at the same shops as his. There is a sort of genius which shows a keen sportsman where he will find plover, and where he will find quail. A higher genius shows to a large and generous man, to a man who knows what life is and how to use it, where to find other men who are worth finding. Sometimes such men are in one place and sometimes in another. Only a fool expects to find them all in satin or in broadcloth. You find Bayard Taylor setting type; you find the artist, Hotchkiss, whom we lost too soon, in a brick-yard; you find Robert Collyer at the anvil; you find Starr King adding up columns at the navy yard; and, if you are wise, you are on the lookout for more hits as happy. I observe a certain lingering interest in America for people of title. Well, an old title ought to mean education, and perhaps good blood; and good blood is one good thing among many. Now it has so happened to me, that the only nobleman of high rank I ever have known well,— the only man whose title ran back to the Emperor Charles,— the only man of that rank who would remember me gladly, and ask me to his house if I travelled that way, is a man whose acquaintance I made when he came to my front door, and asked me if I had an old coat which I could let him have, in place of the rags which had failed him. Now, mark me. I do not say that every man who asks for an old coat is a nobleman in exile. But here was a man who had loved his country better than he loved himself. He had been exiled for the love he bore her; then he had lost his sight in the drudgery in which he had earned his honest bread; and with the same fine feeling and the same literary culture which had become the nobleman, he was living the life of a beggar. His country remembered him afterward, and called him back to his manor and his castle. The man who lives while he lives does not wait, as I did, for chance to bring him such men. He has his eyes open to look for them. I do not say that he seeks his society among beggars. But he does not refuse it when he finds it there.

That is a pretty picture, which has been sketched before now, of the life of a Roman officer in the outpost of Tiberias, one of the most remote outposts of Rome, just eighteen hundred and fifty years ago. I wish one of the masters of imagination would work it out. Imagine the tone of the letters of a fashionable young centurion, transferred from Roman society to this distant garrison,— his complaints that there are no races, no theatre, no society! He describes the tediousness of having to play at dice all day; how soon they exhausted the wretched game of the neighborhood! He ridicules the Jewish customs, and winds up his letter with eager wishes that he may be transferred to Ravenna, or to Marseilles, or to any place but this cursed Tiberias! Such.

groanings unutterable doubtless were uttered in this "cursed Tiberias," at the very hour when Tiberias was one of the places most familiar to the Master of Life, and to his companions who have moulded and moved the world. Words were spoken there then of which the merest fragments are now cherished as oracles; and other words of equal value which are lost, because no man of life stood by with wit enough to write them down. Such officers as this *blasé* centurion jostled in the street Jesus Christ and his comrades. And when he wrote home that life was dull and dark he simply wrote that he was one of the swine who trod pearls under their feet; he wrote that his eye was evil and so his whole body was full of darkness; he wrote, in one word, that he could not live while he lived.

VI. At the bottom of all our sciences and philosophies, of all our reasonings and contrivings, Life is the great secret. The philosopher comes to that, and is silent. The physicist analyzes so far, and here he is defied. We cannot weigh life. We cannot test for it by our re-agents; we cannot measure it by our standards. But between the living man and the dead corpse we know the difference; between dead winter and living summer; between the living violet and the dead sham which the milliner made to resemble it. To use this life, which is our birthright, where we are tempted to put off the use of it,—this is the privilege and duty of the living child of a living God. Imagine some bar of judgment arranged in the theological fancy of the Middle Ages, where some recording angel, half-amused and half-dismayed, is asking you of your career in this world. And what are some of his questionings?

"Boston? You say you lived in Boston?"

"I did, sir."

"Yes, Boston. I remember Boston. I remember there a bay of matchless beauty, a summer sky which the world cannot surpass, long lines of hills sweeping down in weird curves on the west, and on the east the unrhythmed laughter of the infinite ocean. Did you take in the lesson and blessing of all this, every summer day of your life?"

And your answer is, "I beg your pardon. I was occupied in making ready to enjoy it after I should be seventy years old, and alas! I was called away before my preparation had been made."

"Yes? Well:—you are working out in Boston, I remember,

some of the most exquisite problems our Father has given to his children. Education seems to have been trusted to you; the elevation of the Irish seems to have been given to you; the proper government of cities seems to have been consigned to you. What sub-department in these duties did you choose?"

And your answer is, "I beg your pardon, but I must explain again that my daily duty was getting ready to attend to these cares after I was seventy, and unfortunately I was called away too soon."

To which my angel,— "Well, at least, sir, I suppose you could enjoy. You had there galleries of art; you had princes who were only eager to show their pictures, or to lend their books. What use did you make of these? Nay, I see by your record that you had a lovely wife and a household of noble children, thanks to her watchful care. How much time did you spend with them? How much of the joy of home and home's companionship have you taken? Show us at least that you knew how to use the earth, before you ask me to admit you yonder, and to trust you in the life of heaven."

With what face will you stammer for the third time, "I beg your pardon, sir, but I left my home at eight every morning, and I returned to it at eight every night, after my little ones were in bed, because, as I have explained to you, I was all the time getting ready to enjoy these luxuries you have named after I was seventy, and unfortunately I was called away too soon."

VII. To live while we live, is to use life to its very full to-day. The Sermon on the Mount is the code for such life. The life of Jesus Christ, crowded full, is its illustration and its stimulus. For which detailed use of every hour there are plenty of books of reputation.* I am afraid that all of them together are not worth the paper they are written on. It is only the child of God who knows he is child of God, who will seek so to live. And he will find the method, though he cannot read. In simple gratitude to God he will accept the gift, and, as the catechism says, he will live to God's glory, and will enjoy him forever. It is the instinct of a child proud of his father, and determined to live as that father

---

* For instance, Leigh Hunt's essays on these subjects in the *Indicator*, and other series. But I am afraid that these essays are based only on a selfish hypothesis, and speak as if man were a separated or lonely being.

lives, because he is his child. Nor can that man fail to live with all his might, and to gain all this subtle and exquisite joy of life, who recognizes this great companionship in which he lives.

"Let this thought often return, that God fills every place. 'If I ascend into heaven thou art there; if I make my bed in the depths thou art there.' Let, then, everything you see represent to your spirit the presence, the excellency, and the power of God."[*] Often as we cite these grand words we cannot recall them too often: "Let your conversation with the creatures lead you unto the Creator. So shall your actions be done more frequently with an actual eye to God's presence. In the face of the sun you may see God's beauty; in the fire you may feel his heat; in the water his gentleness to refresh you; he it is that comforts your spirits when you have taken cordials. It is the dew of heaven that makes your field give you bread, and the drink to your necessities." "If we walk with God in all his ways, as he walks with us in all ours, we shall find perpetual reasons to rejoice in the Lord always."

Of seeking happiness I say nothing. I am talking of something far more profound, — of the using of life and enjoying the presence of God.

> "Live while you live, the epicure would say
> And seize the pleasures of the passing day.
> Live while you live, the eager preacher cries,
> And give to God each moment as it flies.
> Lord, in thy children's life may both agree:
> We live to pleasure when we live to thee!"[†]

---

[*] Jeremy Taylor, "Holy Living."
[†] After Doddridge. His own lines are somewhat different.

[I will not print this sermon without saying that I am led to prepare it by my memories of the example and stimulus given to all who knew him, by a near friend, who has just now died in Worcester. Of Mr. Theophilus Brown, the first thing which every one said, who knew him, was, "How much good he does find in life!" Of the simplest tastes, he had formed the habit of compelling every hour to bless him as it went by. If you spoke to him of this he would be apt to laugh, and say he had perhaps "caught the knack of living." But it was really more than a "knack"; it was a profound principle. To him the world was a very good world, and he knew how to gain its real good and its infinite treasures, even in things which are foolishly called trifles; and by the same magic he taught younger people how to gain them. He was more than sixty when he died; but in his simple tastes, in his ready companionship, in his enjoyment of every living thing which God had made, he seemed the youngest of the large circle of his friends.]

The sermons already published in this series are —

    THE GREAT HARVEST YEAR,
    LOOKING BACK,
    RITUAL,
    PRAYER,
    RESPECTABILITY,
    YOURSELVES,
    WHAT IT IS TO BE CATHOLIC.

They will be sent by mail, in answer to orders addressed to the Publishers, or to R. B. Palfrey, 12 Garland Street, or Box 3196, Boston Post-office. The price of single sermons is ten cents each; for the series of fifteen, the price is one dollar.

THE ASSOCIATED CHARITIES.

Though I bestow all my goods to feed the poor, and have not charity, it profiteth me nothing.—I. COR. xiii., 3.

It is one of the characteristic traits of civilized men and women that people who live in cities always affect to be very fond of the country, and people who live in the country always hanker for the life of towns. There is, of course, a good deal of affectation in it. If we here really longed for orange-groves, as we pretend to, it is an easy matter to go and plant orange-trees, and we should do it. Or, if we really prized the freedom of Texas or Colorado, as we pretend, why, we should go there. Beneath the affectation, however, there is a healthy feeling, on the side of the city and country both, that each has much to learn from the other. And, as Mr. Olmsted has said, the civilization of our time requires constant effort, both "for the urbanizing of the country and the ruralizing of the cities." The introduction in the country of good roads and walks, conveniences for intercourse, ready purchase and sale, and so on, goes hand in hand with the efforts of cities to open parks, to introduce pure water, to plant living trees instead of dead ones, and to keep them alive when they have been planted. For all such work the best stimulus and guarantee is in the annual ebb and flow, which, every winter, brings into the cities the best of the inhabitants of the country, and every summer carries into the country the best of the inhabitants of the city. The results of such ebb and flow are well shown in England, where country life has more conveniences than anywhere else in the world; and where, on the other hand, even in London, though the largest of cities, the rate of health is better than it is in most even of the smaller cities of the world.

We will consider this morning the lesson which country life has to teach us who live in cities, as to mutual intercourse among people of all classes,— and the good which that intercourse brings about in the largest undertakings of our social life. These results, as achieved in the country towns where they work at most advantage, are such as seem almost miraculous to the jaded social-science student in the city, who sees the "Black Maria" crowded every day, as she takes her sad freight to the House of Correction and the prison, and who reads, every week, of an unchecked mortality far above his desired average. The last summer when I lived in Milton, a town of between two and three thousand people, there was nobody in the poor-house. There was talk of letting rooms in it for summer boarders, the site being exquisite. In winter I think they had four old people in it, who spent their winters there as in a convenient club-house, and in the spring left to visit their friends. In the matter of health, the last report of our Registrar went into a careful argument to show the impossibility of reducing our death-rate here to 14 in the 1000, which some enthusiasts have hoped for (myself among them). But I have only to go fifteen miles, to Canton, to find a town where the death-rate is but 15 in a 1000, with good hope of improvement there. Really, our most enthusiastic plans for improvements in society, which seem in the aggregate fabulous, are little more than the bringing into one view improvements which, in separate detail, have been effected elsewhere. If, for instance, we could introduce here the social conditions of the town of Vineland, in New Jersey, under which they lived for ten years, our police expenses would be twenty-five hundred dollars a year, and our expenses for public charity for our own people "practically nothing." "Practically nothing" is the answer which the relieving officer makes in answer to a question in that direction. All the "public charity" was bestowed on tramps or other wayfarers.

The first great lesson of country life is the advantage the country towns gain because everybody knows everybody. If a man falls off his barn and is killed, and leaves a widow with six children to take care of, everybody knows it and is interested. You might say the whole town, certainly all that neighborhood, becomes a committee of the whole to attend to that woman and her family. Those children do not lack for books at school, for clothes, or for shoes. As they grow up they do not lack for work, and they do not have to carry home shavings and laths for fuel. They are taken right into the common life of the neighborhood. And, at the end of fifty years, probably any one of those children might say that it had been no disadvantage to him, in material affairs, that his father died when he was young. Or as the children study an intelligent boy, eager in books and study, shoots right ahead of his competitors in school. That thoughtful, wise woman, who is the life of the whole village, stops him one day, and bids him come home with her and borrow some books. She makes sure she is right; she knows her boy, and knows that the Commonwealth needs all of such boys it can get. When the time comes she sends him to Harvard College yonder, and pays his bills, though to do so she have to wear the same bonnet and shawl and furs for ten years, and go to church on foot though she used to ride. I could name her name if I dared, and he who is now filling one of the first positions of trust in the Commonwealth would name it, if he were here.

Such chances and such victories are a matter of course in the country. They are not so much crowded there but they can see each others' faces. There is not so much noise but they can hear each others' voices. So they can bear each others' burdens there,— and St. Paul says this is to fulfil the whole law of Christ,— with a certain ease which is impossible here. The consequence is, that in the country towns the crime and even the grinding poverty come from those lonely hovels which are far away from the villages, in unknown "gores," as they call them, in deserts midway between one village and another. They come from these, and from the crowded factory villages, which in a horrid caricature reflect the worst evils of the life of cities. The typical life of old New England rural towns was curiously free both from pauperism and crime.

It is natural enough that people should be distressed with the bitter contrast to all this simple intercourse, which we notice in our life in cities. In your house in town you do not know the boy who brings you your eggs, nor the man who brings you your milk. You do not sit and chat with the cobbler who mends your children's shoes, and you would not know by sight the man who cut and split the wood for your fire. You hardly know what blacksmith shoes your horses, and you would laugh at me if I asked you whether his daughter were in a consumption, or whether he has not a bright boy who ought to be fitted for college. Yet in simple country life you would know all such people and all such things. And true-hearted people and right-minded people are always watching to see how, in the vigor and vitality and high-organization of city life, they can maintain that kindness and loyalty of the life of the country, in which the workman knows his employer and his family, rejoices in their joys, and sorrows in their sorrows; and in which, as well, the employer knows his workman, his joys, and his sorrows, bears them upon his heart, and gives his strength and sympathy. To bring into city life this sense of mutual obligation, to bring back into our society the true meaning of our good old New England word "help," so that each man shall help his brother, as Isaiah says, and every woman her sister,— this is one of the noblest efforts of our time.

The desire to do this has been the central wish of the persons most interested in the plan for associating the charities of Boston, of which you have lately seen some discussions in the journals. A public meeting was held at Chardon Street, last Monday, to carry out their plan. All of us who are interested in the relief of the poor, either personally or professionally, have to be careful that, in our blindness, we do not make paupers of them. And many of us have feared that one hundred and twenty-five different charitable societies, acting each in its own way, with little or no concert, are very apt to do a lasting injury to the manhood of those they relieve, at the very moment in which they confer a temporary solace. To establish a conference, then, between the different societies, and the different churches also, which attempt the relief of the poor, seems one direct step to a more home-like care of them, and to that improvement of the condition of each person relieved which ought to accompany each act of charity. The desire for this union was published fifty years ago by Dr. Joseph Tuckerman. "Can no plan be devised," he says, "for their closer union with each other, or by which they may know what is done by each other, or by the overseers of the poor in the wards in which they severally act?"

From that time to this, numerous efforts have been made in this direction, and with more or less success. But no effort has been made so thorough or so unanimous, or with a plan of organization which seemed so likely to succeed, as that which engages us now. A system is proposed, based upon the large experience of London and of New York, and upon plans which have been tested in detail in Buffalo and in Germantown, which looks, I do not say to a federal union of the charities,— that is too much to ask for,— but to frequent conference, and even toward what our fathers would have called a hundred years ago a confederation. That is to say, that, under this plan, either in ward meetings or in a central meeting, the persons most interested will have an opportunity to meet each other frequently and familiarly, and avoid the dangers of isolated action.

But this association, and the registration which it provides for, are by no means the only objects of the first movers in this plan. They think they can bring about a more genuine intercourse between the rich and the poor, or, if you prefer the name, between the classes which relieve and those which are relieved, in our Boston social order. They have been doing, in one of the North-End wards, exactly what we try to do in our own church charities here. That is, they are not satisfied with sending a modicum of coal or food where it is needed. They try, as we do, to establish personal relationships of confidence and friendship between the adviser and the advised; to divide and subdivide the business of visiting the poor, so that it shall not be an irksome task, but that it can be performed as a sympathetic duty. This is the endeavor. And this relationship, as you see, is to begin again, in city life, on that friendly mutual relation so much easier in the country, in which each helps each, and all can lend a hand. Satisfied, by a trial of the hardest region in Boston, that this can be done there, they believe it can be done, in time, all over the city. And they do not conceal their wish, in calling all the societies to coöperate, that, where the business of charity-visiting has become technical and hard, or where, so far as one can find, no such visits have been made, the several societies may foster a closer and more real relationship between those who give and those who take. Especially their wish is, that the poor may never be classified as the poor, nor become a class of paupers.

The plan of associated charities, then, in proposing a systematic action of all the charitable societies, is specially urged by people who are not satisfied that one City Visitor shall be the only person to see to five hundred families. They hope to quicken all the organizations, so that each of these families may know at least one wise, sympathetic, kindly friend, who may be willing to advise, to encourage, to comfort, to render any service of friendship,— a friend who may be pledged, first of all, and that fanatically, to extricate this family from the unfortunate conditions which compelled them to seek alms.

III. So far as we can permit ourselves here to think of our own separate organization as a church, the plan of the associated charities has no especial interest. It changes not at all the duty and the privilege which this congregation, as a church, holds towards the poverty we find. But our place as a separate church organization is but a matter of minor importance. It is to the Universal Church that we belong, the great family of God; and the value of this little family is nothing, save as it makes us better able to enjoy our joys and do our duties there. And we are glad to have any step taken forward in the gospel work, the work of human tenderness to all God's poor here, and in the business of lifting them out of their poverty.

For years upon years, in our charity work here, we have hoped and tried not to break down the self-respect of those with whom we dealt; we have tried to lift them to more useful life, — to be their real friends in placing them where they should not need our help. Under the wise and tender plans of Miss Tallant, who understood the problems of poverty so well, while she relieved its sorrows so sweetly, the arrangements made in the "South Friendly" for the sympathetic care which I have tried to describe, seem to embody all that tenderness could ask, and wisdom could plan, to unite sympathy and intelligence in the union which on Monday Mr. Brooks was pleading for so earnestly. What we of to-day have to do is, to infuse into such plans the divine spirit of love, and to carry them out with the personal eagerness which defies routine, which treats each sufferer as if his case were wholly new, and which refuses to be disconcerted by failure or by ingratitude. Of what we can do in this spirit I have tried to sketch the picture, by reminding you of those simple intimacies and perpetual kindnesses of country life.

The district assigned to our church takes in the region between the Albany Railroad and Newton Street, bounded on the west by Tremont Street. It seems that in that region there are some forty Protestant families in need of more or less outside relief through the winter months, to whom we can be of special service. Generally this is in the simple form of giving from the sewing-room down stairs a parcel of plain needle-work every week, for which the work-woman is paid the next week. Her work is superintended, and if, when the winter begins, she cannot do it well, she has a chance to learn how with those who are willing to teach. The greatest pride of the ladies charged with this work is, to have one of their work-women leave them for higher wages. With these forty families, some one or other of us is on friendly terms. I do not think there would be sickness in one of these homes, and we here ignorant of it. I do not think a boy would be placed at his trade or a girl sent to a new school, and some of us not consulted. So far, then, we have here the entering wedge for that sort of intimacies, which I have tried to describe, in which you level up a family, though it be that of the poorest widow in Boston, and make yourself sure that you are not adding to a permanent caste or class of paupers. In such intimacies we ought not to be in the least satisfied that there is coal and oatmeal enough in store to carry a family through a week. That is the duty, and a duty, and a very noble duty, of the official alms-giver. But that duty does not satisfy the Christian friend. We want to see that the boys and girls in such families have good amusements rather than bad,— that they read good books and not vulgar and debasing ones. We should watch with them if they were sick, and provide them medicines. But we should much prefer to watch with them before they are sick, and provide preventions. If the lodgings are behind a liquor shop, and the children exposed to temptation, the girls to insult, we are glad to move them away. If the boy "gets a place," as they say, as bar-tender, we ought to be on the look-out to put him at better work,— to have one bar-tender the less in the world, and one blacksmith, or, better, one farmer, the more. When the happy time comes when one widowed mother finds out that Meander Street or Harrison Avenue is not the best place to bring up her children, we ought to know where is the town on the hill-sides of New England, or in the midst of Western luxury, where she and they are needed. My excellent friend, Mr. Bradley, in the midst of the varied work of his Heath Street Chapel, — a church which worships in a railway station,— found time and means in two years to forward, or to help in forwarding, forty sets of emigrants, many of them with their families, from crowded Roxbury to the waiting West. Our flour and beef are the cheaper for every such migration ; and for the children of these families, this means health instead of puny struggle,— real wealth instead of grinding penury,— life abundant instead of living death. It is impossible to go into much detail. But in the word friendship, rather than condescension, the whole is implied. The object is not feeding the poor,— it is their elevation from poverty. I can well understand that you might do a boy more good by giving him a concert ticket than by giving him a jacket. The gift of the jacket might make a pirate of him,— he might never earn another jacket. The gift of the concert ticket might quicken the best tastes God had given him,— might determine him to tread under foot temptations which surrounded him,— might give him the feeling of companionship with those he knew were his superiors, and determine him that he also would give such pleasures some day to others. Open to boy or girl, in an evening spent with them, the art of reading. I mean, show them how to use and how to choose among books which you now lay so lavishly before them. In that evening, it may be that you have saved boy or girl from temptations thrust before them at every corner,— that you have opened up a vista which leads even to infinite life. Mrs. Farnham, one of the John Howards of our times, whose work in prisons and for prisoners has blessed Europe and America, used to say that she was started from the dead inaction of the poorest wilderness life, when a kind traveller gave her a copy of De Witt Clinton's speeches. I can well believe it, because he was a *kind* traveller, and meant well to the lonely girl he found starving for something more than she found in carding wool, in spinning flax, or in feeding hens.

Every boy who is trained to depend on begging from door to door is one more pirate thrown into the community, to be watched and caught and imprisoned and discharged, and watched and caught again, and imprisoned and discharged again, in one long dreary series of wretchedness, till it pleases God to release him from a world which has been too much for him, and to try him in another. Every boy, on the other hand, whom you lift from that grade of beggary, who comes to respect himself and to determine to rise in honor as in work, is a child of God, to whom you have revealed himself. He is so much gain to the Commonwealth and to God's service in the world. Nor is this slight service. He deserves well of God and man who makes two blades of grass grow where one grew before. Of how much higher desert is he or she who, from a wilderness hopeless and dead, rescues these little ones, who to the next generation are to be men and women, pure, godly, brave, and true! And there is not one of us who may not enlist in such service. I heard it said, the other day, that the tender care of the poor of Boston, such as I have described, would require two thousand Florence Nightingales. That is quite true. What shame to Boston,— what shame to the religion which builds these churches, which paints their walls with saints, which bids those walls echo with harmonies of song or of prayer,—if we have not two thousand, and ten times two thousand, women here fit to do all that St. Florence herself could do, in this work of lifting up those that are fallen down. Simply to take one widow poorer than yourself into the sympathy of friendship, simply to make one half-starved drunkard's wife sure of one loyal friend, simply to carry into a tenement lodging-house the neatness and order and discipline which to your own home give that sacred name of home, simply in one such home to do unto others what you would have others do unto you! No, there is no lack of women for such enterprises, thoughtful and unselfish, nor of men, prompt, considerate, and brave.

And I will not for an instant speak as if only the poor, as we call them, received the blessing, and the rich, as we call them, gave it. If it were only a five-dollar bill which you put into the offertory or the charity-box, forgotten in the hour, the mere tribute of accidental good-nature, that might be so. But when you give yourself, when you think out this problem of perplexity, when you sacrifice your own comfortable evening to making yonder home less dreary, when, by your teaching, that boy becomes less stupid and more able to bear his burdens, then you begin to find what the Master meant, "Blessed are the merciful, for they shall obtain more power for mercy." Live outside yourself, and you begin to find what life, unbounded and abundant, is. We need not plead, indeed, so much for those poor who are not here. For ourselves when we are mean or selfish, for ourselves when we have nothing we are willing to give away, for ourselves when we think our comfort is the first object in the universe, we may well plead at the throne of grace. That God will open our eyes! That God will kindle our hearts! That he will teach us to bear each others' burdens! For we also are the poorest of the poor, if we do not learn to pour forth, and that boldly, from that which has been given to our keeping. "Let us not love in word nor in tongue, but in deed and in truth." Thus shall we know what it is to be sons and daughters of God.

To return to that comparison of the openness of country life, and the close imprisonment of cities, let me read Cowper's bitter lines, not yet a hundred years old. I think they are the only verses in which he alludes to the dismemberment of the British Empire, in which America was lost to the English crown. It is worth notice that he ascribes the folly of the administration of the time — and he was right — to the folly and selfishness of London : —

   She has her praise. Now mark a spot or two
That so much beauty would do well to purge,
And show this queen of cities that so fair
May yet be foul; so witty, yet not wise.
It is not seemly nor of good report
That she is slack in discipline; more prompt
To avenge than to prevent the breach of law.
That she is rigid in denouncing death
On petty robbers, and indulges life,
And liberty, and ofttimes honors, too,
To peculators of the public gold! . . .
Advancing Fashion to the post of Truth,
And centering all authority in modes
And customs of her own, till Sabbath rites
Have dwindled into unrespected forms,
And knees and hassocks are well-nigh divorced.

God made the country, and man made the town;
What wonder, then, that health . . .
  . . . should most abound
And least be threatened in the fields and groves?
  . . . We [here] can spare
The splendor of your lamps. . . .
  . . . Your songs confound
Our more harmonious notes. The thrush departs,
Scared, and the offended nightingale is mute.
There is a public mischief in your mirth, —
It plagues your country. Folly such as yours,
Graced with a sword, and worthier of a fan,
Has made — what enemies could ne'er have done —
Our arch of Empire, steadfast but for you,
A mutilated structure, soon to fall.

The sermons already published in this series are —

**THE GREAT HARVEST YEAR,
LOOKING BACK,
RITUAL,
PRAYER,
RESPECTABILITY,
YOURSELVES,
WHAT IT IS TO BE CATHOLIC,
THE JOY OF LIFE.**

They will be sent by mail, in answer to orders addressed to the Publishers, or to R. B. Palfrey, 12 Garland Street, or Box 3196, Boston Post-office. The price of single sermons is ten cents each; for the series of fifteen, the price is one dollar.

10

THE REVISION OF THE BIBLE.

The righteousness which is of faith speaketh on this wise:
"The word is nigh thee, in thy mouth and in thy heart; that is, the word of faith which we preach." — ROMANS x., 6-8.

Nine years ago, in February, 1870, the Convocation of Canterbury, which represents the largest part of the Church of England, proposed a revision of the Bible, as it is read in churches, in all English-speaking lands. In September, 1870, the work in England began. A part of the plan proposed that a body of scholars in America should carry on the work contemporaneously with the English Commission. Such a board was appointed and began its work in 1872. I remember speaking here of the enterprise soon after, and trying to show what was the class of difficulties in Scripture reading which it might be hoped it would remove. What I said then I printed at the time, and I do not return to that subject now; for the work is so nearly done that we may soon test the fruits for ourselves. Let me try to tell you briefly what has been done by way of preparation for the day, not very distant, when I shall be reading here from a Bible more accurate than I have ever read from here before.

The American Commission made what I may call its report of progress at a large meeting held in this city on Thursday last. The meeting was itself a historic occasion. From distant parts of the country had come together these scholars, whose skill in the languages has given them the distinguished privilege of weighing again the words which, in an English tongue, shall represent the old Hebrew and Chaldee and Greek. To meet them had been summoned presidents and professors in colleges, a large number of the clergy of all communions, and of distinguished gentlemen in other callings, all interested in knowing what is to be this rendering of those Scriptures, on which, in so large measure, depend our written laws, and so much of our religious and social order. Seven of the gentlemen concerned in the work of revision explained the method and object of that work, in addresses made to this assembly; and then, by spokesmen of authority, the meeting expressed its profound interest in the undertaking. This interest was expressed in other ways indeed, and there can be no doubt that the best scholarship and thought of the United States and of England are in sympathy with this endeavor to improve the popular knowledge of the Scriptures.

At this meeting it was announced that the work of the English Commission on the New Testament is in substance finished. It only awaits the incorporation of the suggestions of the American Commission on some of Paul's Epistles. It would perhaps be possible to print it within a year, unless its publication be deferred to the completion of the Old Testament. The Old Testament work is the more slow, and there is more of it. It will not be finished probably for two years. There are some reasons for deferring the publication of the New Testament to the completion of the Old. It would be well, for instance, if, in the citation of a psalm or a prophecy in the New Testament, the words should be the same in both parts of the Bible. This is not so, as the Bible stands, and, of course, a certain inconvenience follows.

I. The enterprise in hand is not a new translation of the Bible into the language of to-day. That Divine Law which men now call "natural selection," and now "Providence," has so ordered history that the English Bible is the noblest monument of the English language. It was translated by martyrs, men who took their lives in their hands that they might translate it. That gave movement and energy to its words of Infinite Life. It took its present form in the young, exuberant life of the English language, when, as has been well said, men were using the language with the joy of discoverers,— in the time which made immortal Spenser, and Sidney, and Bacon, and Shakspeare. Our timid days, our life in the purple or the palace, our critical weighing of words, will never give us the flow of language or the power of speech which men had then. We know too well to think that we can write better prose than Bacon, better poetry than Shakspeare, or clothe Isaiah in words more divine than some unknown poet chose for Isaiah in this book, or write narrative more pure than that in which Wiclif and Tyndale and Coverdale clothed Matthew's Gospel. The translation, in its form and dialect, is to be retained. Even the method of language, though it seem quaint, is to be preserved in any corrections. No word is to be used in it not in our Bible now. What we make is, not a new translation, but a revision of that we had before. We retain the "thees" and the "thous." We retain the Saxon conciseness and quaintness. We retain "Thus saith the Lord." We retain every syllable of the Lord's Prayer, and, I think, every word of the Ten Commandments. I once tried the experiment of reading here ten or twelve verses of the New Testament in Bishop Ellicott's specimen of the revision. The passage was not a specially familiar one, though not unfamiliar. I think no person in this congregation knew of the change till I told them; so that no sensibilities need be shocked as to the degree or bad taste of the proposed alteration.

It is by revision, indeed, not by new translation, that the English Bible became what it is. The first work, practically, was by Wiclif, more than a hundred years before Columbus discovered America. Decade by decade, generation by generation, men improved on his version. The fatal idea of a finished or even an authorized version did not exist in those times. The art of printing gave new zeal to translators. The Reformation quickened them to passionate enthusiasm. They learned Hebrew and Greek more carefully, that they might better render the Scripture. And, as I have said, their own language was taking on the perfect symmetry and the exquisite beauty of its maiden youth. From the time of Wiclif, in 1380, till King James's version, as we call it, was printed in 1611,— a period of more than two centuries,— this process of correction went steadily on. With every generation, the danger of mistake to the English reader was diminished,—

"Fine, by degrees, and beautifully less."

In certain minor matters, indeed, this revision has gone forward ever since. The proof-readers, or correctors of the press, have taken liberties which no law permitted, but common-sense has justified. Obsolete words have given place to modern spelling under their eye. Thus, "moe" becomes "more," "causey" becomes "causeway," "aliant" becomes "alien," he "neesed" becomes he "sneezed," at the simple discretion of the printers. But such discretion varies; so that, in another place, you may find the obsolete word unchanged. The first edition of King James substituted the black word Judas for the loved name of Jesus, in one unfortunate passage. The error was corrected in the next, but no like authority has been sufficient to correct other errors as gross, till now.

II. Failing any authority for gradual correction, there has accumulated, in two and a half centuries of human progress, much knowledge on the Scripture which ought to be incorporated in the people's Bible, but is still shut up as the peculiar possession of scholars.

1. We know the text of the New Testament much better than men knew it in the seventeenth century. The translators of King James's time used a Greek Testament printed by Erasmus. We know now that this was based on manuscripts comparatively late and not very accurate. The worst story of its inaccuracy is in the fact that there is one passage where Erasmus himself wrote the Greek,— the last six verses of the Revelations,— translating them from the Latin back to Greek, because they were lost from his manuscript. Perhaps from mere convenience to the printer, he made the basis of his work one of the latest manuscripts he had, belonging to the sixteenth century. In place of this,— for a single instance of our many resources,— we can now compare twenty-six uncial manuscripts, as they are called, running from the fourth century to the tenth, of which Erasmus never saw but one, and that one he did not use. We have the diligent and almost fanatical study which the same centuries have given to the ancient versions into other languages, and to the quotations made by the earliest fathers of the Church. We are thus able to speak with a very near approach to substantial certainty, not literal precision, as to the words written by Paul, Luke, Mark, and the rest. I should say that there is not left a single important passage where scholars have any real doubt as to the drift of the language first employed. Of course the variation in detail is endless; but so great was the care always taken by copyists, that these variations do not often strike at very critical or important subjects of discussion.*

2. I have been speaking of the Greek text of the New Testament. Within narrower limits, I may say that we have also a somewhat better Hebrew text of the Old Testament than the translators of King James had. What is much more

---

* I append at the close of this sermon an illustration of this statement from the Sermon on the Mount.

important, men know Hebrew vastly better than they knew it then. They had then only such a knowledge as the Jews of their time had, such a knowledge as a man brings home of the conversational language of a country he has travelled in. Men have now a careful scientific knowledge of Hebrew. They have studied it in its relations with Arabic, with which it is almost as closely connected as is Italian with Latin, and in its relations with other languages of the same family. Now the translators of King James's time knew Greek very well. We have, therefore, a good Greek translation of a careless text of the New Testament. But the men who translated the Old Testament did not know Hebrew very well. We have, therefore, in King James's Bible, not a very good translation of what was quite a good text of the Old Testament. The revision will show, for these reasons, many more important changes in the language of the Old Testament than in that of the New.

III. Next to this fundamental matter — what shall they translate — comes the question, "Who shall translate, or who shall revise?"

This matter has been admirably well arranged, with much more ease than could have been thought possible. The Convocation of Canterbury represents the largest section of the English Church,— a sort of conference of the clergy, without political power, but with great moral and advisory power, when it has a chance to act. In February, 1870, this Convocation proposed the new revision, and, loyal to truth, rising quite above lines of sect, proposed it should be entrusted to scholars of every communion. It was afterwards arranged that a body of American scholars should make an auxiliary commission, to work, on this side of the water, side by side with the Commission in England, and that the two Commissions should interchange results, acting on the same general plan. This broad scheme has been happily carried out. Every leading branch of the English-speaking Church is represented.* The English Commission consists of fifty-two scholars; the American,— which was named on our side, by representative men and scholars,— of twenty-six. The reputations of men of classical and Hebrew scholarship do not generally travel far outside the circle of their immediate readers; but in this company are some names well known

---

* Our own communion, by Mr. Vance Smith, in England, and Professor Abbot, here. Nor could we ask for representatives more creditable.

in general literature. Such are the names, in Great Britain, of Alford and Wilberforce, no longer living ; of Dean Stanley, Archbishop Trench, Dr. Wordsworth, and Bishops Ellicott and Lightfoot. With us, the names of Dr. Schaff, of Dr. Stowe, of Dr. Warren, Professor Abbot, and Dr. Thayer will be generally known. The only danger in such a selection is, that the mood of the scholar, with its sharp, hard accuracy, may be too much for the stress and life of the poet, always more true, though less angular. Now the Bible is preëminently a book of poetry, and it always has proved, in this world, that the insight of the poet is worth more for truth than the precision of the rabbi. To have made either Commission quite perfect, the British Commission should have remembered the value of good English as well as good Hebrew, and given seats to Tennyson and Gladstone, as we might do to Bryant and Longfellow. But, in a revision which owes so much to Dr. Stanley's care, everything is to be hoped ; and, though it early lost Dr. Alford, it is known that his spirit guided the selection of his associates.

IV. This is not the place for a description of the method of work. The two Commissions, separated by the ocean, have worked independently, each in two companies,— an Old Testament and a New Testament company,— and have exchanged, confidentially, in print, their results. A little incident, narrated on Thursday, shows how thorough is the work on each side. It so happened that the two Commissions exchanged their first drafts of the Epistle to the Hebrews, each sending its note without having seen the other's. When the English text arrived here, it proved that the Commission had made nine hundred and thirteen changes in our present version. Of these, four hundred and seventy-six had been already suggested in the same identical words, by their American brethren, without concert with them. A similar coincidence was observed by the Old Testament companies, when they exchanged, in the same way, the prophecy of Isaiah.

Under such auspices, it is now announced that the New Testament is in substance completed, after a constant work of ten years. It only needs the last work of the American revisers, and the consideration of their criticisms in England. It may be that the New Testament may be printed so that we may use it in this pulpit in another year. The Old Testament, from its length, and from intrinsic difficulties, requires more time. Two years more will be requisite to complete it.

When finished, the new revision will not be introduced by any authority. The days of such authority are over. Even our present Bible was never introduced by authority. The translators were appointed by King James; they did their work, and the universities printed it. That was all. It was the best English Bible, and in time people bought it. But if it were not the best, it would not be used. If it were not the best to-day, it would not be read from this pulpit; and when a better best comes, that better best will take its place, not by any leap, not by any command, but as any new edition takes the place of an older edition,— as men read Bryant's *Iliad* more than they read Chapman's, even though there are many lines better in Chapman than there are in Bryant. The Earl of Shaftesbury, in a foolish attack on the revision, said that it was an effort by synodical interference to destroy all the existing Bibles in the world. I might as well say that the Waltham Watch Company was an effort by corporate interference to destroy all the existing watches in the world. If the Waltham watch prove the best, careful people will carry it. Gradually old watches will wear out, and then those who use them will buy new ones. But watch or Bible will be known by its fruits. There is no other test in earth; no, nor in heaven!

I have no hesitation in prophesying that, in a generation, the revised Bible will be in ninety-nine out of a hundred of the pulpits of English-speaking Christendom. I have none in saying that it will be in this pulpit the day that it can first be brought to Boston, if I am that day the servant of this church,— as I hope to be. "That more light and more truth are coming out of God's Holy Word,"— by that prophecy John Robinson consecrated New England the day of her birth and baptism. "More light and more truth,"— to that prophecy New England has held up the country, forced it up, when necessary, in the crash of battle and by the arbitrament of war. "To more light and more truth," is all our liberal Christian movement pledged. And this church would cease to be, if she ceased to proclaim the same word of promise.

"From God's Holy Word, more light, more truth, and more!"

V. At the same time, it is true that we have not the same sort of interest in this great enterprise which our friends of other communions feel. We have learned what they seem to have yet to learn, that "the letter killeth and only the spirit giveth life." If the spirit of man is true enough and wise enough and has light enough from God to sit in judgment on two texts in two parchments, and decide which of them is better than the other, then is it true that the "spirit of man is the candle of the Lord." Our fathers have bravely gone through this business of analyzing the written word, and finding the value of its jots and of its tittles. We have entered into their work, and ought to be grateful to them, that they have done it for us so well as they have. To us the "Word of God" is what it was to St. John,—every expression of God's will and his power. To us it is true that he smiles in the sunbeam, it is true that he speaks in the tempest, it is true that his handwriting is over all the world. "He never left himself without a witness in that he did good." Of his dealings with Israel in her days of idolatry and weakness, we are glad to have Israel's record. Of his revelation of himself in Jesus Christ, we are glad to have the record made by Christ's disciples. But, in either case, these are the records of a revelation and not the revelation itself. And while we are adjusting and readjusting words and phrases, we can never impudently assert for our own work, when it is done, that this is a faultless and unique oracle of the Word of God!

Nor do I make this proud claim for our handful of churches only. We must look on this whole enterprise of revision as a final death-blow to that idolatry of the Bible, in all Protestant churches, which paralyzed the first triumphs of the Reformation, and has so benumbed religion for these later centuries. In the midst of the first true enthusiasm of "justification by faith," men were stopped by their leaders, as if they were told that God had forgotten his world, that he had gone on a journey, like Baal, and had left behind him a finished book, as his last will and testament for mankind. This book they were to worship as if it had been a stone which fell from heaven. That worship of word and letter has benumbed Christendom while it lasted. For there cannot be the pure religion of the Spirit, when men are bending all their energy to construe the enigmas of an oracle. Of that idolatry, I say the end has come now. For men do not take their idol from its shrine, and polish it, and clean it, insert a new jewel in this eye, and trim down the fold of that lock of hair, if they mean to fall down and worship it when once more it stands upon the pedestal. In the course of the discussions of the revision, I have heard one learned man of an evangelical school say, with charming simplicity, that he supposed all his hearers knew that it was only the consonants of the Old Testament Hebrew which were directed by the inspiration of God, but that the vowels, appended to these consonants, are simply the uninspired work of man. When we come to as fine a point as that,—inspired consonants and uninspired vowels,—the whole idolatry of the letter is of course tumbling to its fall. After eighteen centuries the indignant protest of Jesus Christ against the worship of the letter will begin to have its sway, and will really enter into the understandings of men.

From this time forth, as I believe, we may look for another advance — slow but sure — of the religion of life. To know that people and preacher have one Bible, is a help to that religion. The secrets which learned men have known about this book are henceforth to be the property of him that runs. So much is gained. More than this, the mock mystery surrounding it is over. Men will read it for what it is. Better than this, and more, it will be help and not hindrance. The noblest voice of the ages to the children of God, it will speak to them now to assert their relationship to him, to bid them listen to all his voices, and to enter into his work. "Where two or three are gathered together in my name, there am I in the midst of them." "I will send you another comforter, who shall abide with you forever." "The Word is nigh thee, in thy heart and in thy mouth." "Why not of your own selves judge ye what is right?" These are the promises, the encouragements, the directions. And man, the Son of God as he is, life from God's life, inspired by his Spirit, will use every word spoken here to the fathers; will use every word written yonder in the sunbeam or on the snow-flake; will hearken as well to every whisper of his own true heart; and will interpret every oracle spoken in the Gentile history of mankind. The Word of God shall have full course. The leaf shall be for fruit and the root for medicine. And so, with every day of every year, shall man come nearer to God.

So, with every day of every year, shall God's kingdom come!

THE PROBABLE REVISION.

To illustrate the similarity between the approved text and that to which we are accustomed, I read the following passage from Bishop Ellicott's statement of the probable results of revision. It will be observed that it differs from the English of our Bibles in only three passages.

"And seeing the multitudes he went up into the mountain, and when he was set, his disciples came unto him. And he opened his mouth and taught them, saying, —

"Blessed *are* the poor in spirit: for theirs is the kingdom of heaven. Blessed *are* they that mourn: for they shall be comforted. Blessed *are* the meek: for they shall inherit the earth. Blessed *are* they that hunger and thirst after righteousness: for they shall be filled. Blessed *are* the merciful: for they shall obtain mercy. Blessed *are* the pure in heart: for they shall see God. Blessed *are* the peacemakers: for they shall be called the sons of God. Blessed are they which are persecuted for righteousness' sake: for theirs is the kingdom of heaven. Blessed are ye when men shall revile you, and persecute you, and shall say all manner of evil against you falsely, for my sake. Rejoice and be exceeding glad, for great is your reward in heaven: for so persecuted they the prophets which were before you."

I do not mean to say that these three variations fairly illustrate the importance of the variations which will be made by the revision. I cited this passage rather for the purpose of showing that the most familiar passages of the Testament are, by a very natural law, those in which the least variation is made by copyists.

No person is yet at liberty to state publicly what are the results of the commission. But Bishop Ellicott, whose authority is very high, has given this illustration of the "probable revision."

The sermons already published in this series are —

> THE GREAT HARVEST YEAR,
> LOOKING BACK,
> RITUAL,
> PRAYER,
> RESPECTABILITY,
> YOURSELVES,
> WHAT IT IS TO BE CATHOLIC,
> THE JOY OF LIFE,
> THE ASSOCIATED CHARITIES.

They will be sent by mail, in answer to orders addressed to the Publishers, or to R. B. Palfrey, 12 Garland Street, or Box 3196, Boston Post-office. The price of single sermons is ten cents each; for the series of fifteen, the price is one dollar.

11

THE BIBLE.

Many other signs did Jesus, which are not written in this book; but these are written, that ye might believe, and that believing ye might have life in his name. If they should be written every one, I suppose that the world itself should not contain the books that should be written.
—JOHN xx., 30, 31 ; xxi., 25.

In the Bible itself there is no reference to the Bible.
There is reference to the "Book of the Law," and the Saviour once and again speaks of "the Law and the Prophets." Here he alludes to the books read in the Jewish meeting-houses of his time. Of these, all parties respected the Law as containing the historical and constitutional basis of the national existence of Israel; while the Prophets,—including what we know as the Psalms, the Proverbs, and the book of Job, were held in varied respect by different sects. The Pharisees had also an enthusiasm of their own for the traditions, written and unwritten, which had come down to them regarding the interpretation of the Law. These, however, were only the notions of the Jews. The Christian Church, at its very birth, abridged the Jewish Law, into the mere statement that Christians must abstain from meats offered to idols, from fornication, from things strangled, and "from blood," the last cautions having special reference to the heathen sacrifice and custom of the time. And, in all the correspondences and all the legislation of the Early Church, in Christ's own words,—be it remarked especially,—there is no reference to any book, written form, written code, or scripture of any kind. Paul's phrase to a divinity student, Timothy, often quoted with a false significance, that "all scripture is given for edification," is simply an exhortation to the young man to read anything he could find. In that day of few books, he could get good, Paul said, out of everything. It is a remark which Paul would certainly not make to-day, with regard to all the writings or publications of our time. But, considering how desirable it is that a young preacher should study, and how apt he is to prefer not to study, but to inflict his own wisdom on his

hearers, and how little danger there was that Timothy would be misled in his reading, there is no wonder that Paul told him that all that there was then in writing, Latin, Greek, or Hebrew, was meant for edification, and would probably do him more good than harm. The writing of books with intent to kill had not then begun.

The Bible, then, holds the central place which it now occupies in the affection and respect of the Church of Christ, from certain intrinsic merits of its own, which can probably be ascertained by examination. It does not depend on any authoritative direction of Christ, or of any of its own writers, for acceptance and regard.

Christ, on the other hand, left the Christian Commonwealth, from age to age, under the direction of the Holy Spirit. Each age was to find out by its best prayer and struggle what God himself wanted it to do, and the Saviour certified and guaranteed that each age might trust confidently to that ever-present Word. As to that criticism by which the Jews of his time analyzed their own law, and took away such life as it had in their vivisection, he always spoke of that with contempt. "The letter kills, only the spirit gives life," he says. In face of such discouragement of a pedantic and literal interpretation of the Bible, this collection of history, prophecy, poetry, and precept, wholly unlike anything else existing, even in its literary form, holds, by its own moral power, a central place in the Church and in civilization. It is a place often challenged, bitterly and fiercely; now intelligently challenged, and now stupidly. Nay, it is a position seldom intelligently defended. The friends of the Christian religion have said and done few things as absurd as in their eager defence of the Bible. For all this, however, in spite of bitter attack and in spite of foolish defence, the Bible, of its own moral force and vitality, holds its position. At this moment it is the book most widely known in the world, the book most eagerly studied, the book which exercises the most profound control over the characters of men, and of course over the destiny of nations. The Roman Catholic Church, in the most serious mistake of administration which it was ever lured into, undertook, at one period of its history, to set the weight of Bible instruction below its own, by way of giving more dignity to its own decisions. But the Roman Church long since discovered that error, and in our own time is as fond, I think, of citing Biblical authority or Biblical illustrations for its claims as are

the men of any communion. Certainly it has furnished, within this century, some keen and intelligent critics, both for the text and the meaning of the Bible. The Protestant Church at its birth undoubtedly fell into the counter error which has well been called Biblio-latry,— the worship of a book. This Biblio-latry found its most celebrated expression in Chillingworth's often-repeated epigram:—
"The Bible, and the Bible only, is the religion of Protestants."
But this epigram wholly understates the vitality or infinity of pure religion. God, in his children and in his Spirit, is the religion of Protestants, as of all Christians; nor should any narrower statement, even in enthusiastic reverence for the Bible itself, take the place of truth so broad and simple.

The Bible holds its place, none the less, in face of the assaults of enemies, of the follies of friends, and in spite of the indifference of the careless. It holds its place, not because Christ or Paul or John appealed to it, for they did not; not because the Church of Rome once disowned it, and afterward readopted it; not because the Protestant Church once made it an idol; not because the claim can be maintained that every word in it is literally or plenarily inspired. It retains its place from certain central and essential moral forces of its own, which distinguish it from other agencies acting on man or society.

It is worth while to name the more important of these in their order:—
I. First, then: the Bible is not an accidental collection, but the best result of the religious aspiration of the ages and nations in which it was formed.
The suggestion is often made in our time, that it would be an enterprise of real value to select another Bible from the religious writings of all nations,— of which it is carelessly said that there are a great many which compare not unfavorably with this Bible. But such selections are, in fact, going on all the time,— always have been going on. Literature is simply such refining and selection. The Sibylline Books of Rome were a celebrated selection of this kind. The esoteric writings of the Egyptians were a selection of this kind. Such selections always will be going on. It is popularly forgotten, I think, that the Bible itself is just such a selection. It is a selection made by exactly the law which the naturalist

Darwin calls the Law of Natural Selection, in which the strongest maintains its being in a struggle for life, and the weakest goes to the wall and dies. The Bible is a selection which was some two thousand years making itself, by that very law, from unnumbered prophecies, poems, precepts, histories, and letters. That which, on the test of those two thousand years, proved valuable for the eternal life of man, proved indeed invaluable,— lived. It got itself preserved in one canon or another, sifted out from chaff, and kept by the gratitude of people, who had found in it help and blessing. The little scraps of Hebrew history are mere specimen pages from volume upon volume of annals, chronicles, legends, and poems unnumbered, which have gone to their own place. The Psalms, only one hundred and fifty of them, are what were saved, century in and century out, from all the religious lyrics of the people most inclined to worship who have ever lived, whose worship involved the singing of such lyrics, and their composition, constantly. Of fifteen hundred years of such worship, there are preserved one hundred and fifty little poems, more than half of them from the inspiration of one man, the first lyric poet of all time. So of the prophecies. The orators of that people,— nay, their statesmen, their leaders of whatever kind,— uttered these eager invocations, appeals, warnings, parables, in which they illustrated God's presence and power. Of hundreds of their prophets, we have not one word. Of hundreds, nay thousands, more, we have not word nor name. Of all, we have a few fragmentary addresses by fifteen or sixteen men. Are these addresses preserved by mere accident? Not at all. They are preserved in stress of war and exile and agony,— the selected gems from other collections which had been kept in other stress of war and exile and agony,— which were what men could not part with, though in war and exile and agony, from the religious literature of warning and appeal of their country. So of the book of Job. One solitary monument of all the religious literature of a thousand years, of a race of men larger than the Hebrew race, and cultivated, as the book itself shows! From all its work of worship and religion,— the law of natural selection, thinning down and thinning down, held on to this poem, the choice and peculiar poem, which could not be lost or thrown away.

Precisely the same is true of the New Testament. Plenty of letters, of course, from Paul and other apostles. But these are those which were so well worth preserving and copying, fighting for, dying for, that these survived while the others are gone. Plenty of tales of Jesus in that first century, written here, written there. But here were four memoirs, standing test, rising above their fellows, better authenticated, more full of life. By the law of natural selection, these live while the others die.

This is always to be remembered when people talk glibly of selections from the religious literature of all nations,— that the Bible is such a selection from selections from selections. The Old Testament is the quintessence, the fifth power, of the religious literature of the most religious race on earth; the New Testament is the select few of the memoirs of apostolic time, which, in the early ages, survived persecution, survived scepticism, survived error and criticism, so as to maintain their own essential place as the most important memoirs of the most important event in the history of man.

II. Second. The favor with which the Bible is received by our European races, is in part the welcome they give, like a thirsty man's to water, to the Oriental habit of thought and language, which, in essence, are so much nobler and truer than our own. It is to this that we owe it, that, as Mr. Martineau says, "The Pharaohs are less strangers to our people at large than the Plantagenets, and Abraham is more distinct than Alfred."

The native habits of thought and the habits of expression of the Western or European races are of what Mr. Dickens calls the Gradgrind sort. They are apt to look at things merely in their mechanical relations. To their view, the use of the cataract is to turn a mill; and the use of virtue is to make the house neat, and to put good things to eat on the table. Yet this is no more natural to the soul of man than it is natural to the Indian to go for two days without food. Put your new-killed venison before him, and he will show you whether his abstinence was "natural." Put your Oriental Bible, with its enthusiasm for the soul of man, for God and unseen realities, for right, truth, heaven, for beauty and loving kindness,— put this before your mechanical clodhopper of Wales or of Glasgow, of Eisenach, or of the Ober Amergau, or of New Lebanon here,— yes, or of Boston, or New York, or Chicago,— and see how it will satisfy a part of his being which none of your machinery has fed! It is to the peculiarity of race which I have indicated, that it is due, that the Bible has its most enthusiastic admirers in Western lands. The Western missionary carries it back to Persia, or even to India, and is disappointed, when, with all concession of respect for the wisdom and even truth of its contents, he cannot obtain enthusiasm for its form and language equal to that which is gained at his home. He has carried it to regions where men are used to look at the soul as substance, and not shadow; at men and God as the rulers of the elements, and not their slaves.

And we may safely say that God himself, in the providential training of the world, has meant that the great Eastern races should train us in faith, in the basis of all poetry, invention, and philosophy, as that we should train them in organization, in method, civil order, and the combinations of material things. We may well afford to send to them our constitutions, our manufacture, the books of our printing and the cloths of our loom, if, in the providence of God, they send us the vision of seer and the word of prophet; teach us the syllables of our prayer and lend us the language of our hymns. It is one instance more, in God's great work, of the way in which men bear each others' burdens. It is what St. Paul, an "Easterner," speaking to "Westerners" of Rome, calls "the mutual faith of you and me." *

III. This is, however, but a local peculiarity, though a peculiarity which covers more than half the world. For the whole world the Bible asserts a distinction, which we feel, even when we do not analyze it, in the impersonality of the authors,— a characteristic not to be claimed for every line of their work, but still a dominant of the whole. There is none of the figure-posing of our modern literature, which in this resembles our modern pallet. There is none of that smirk which comes in at the balanced end of a remarkable performance, with the brazen inquiry, " Have I not done that well?" Indeed, there is no performance at all. Solidly, very briefly, and with an intensity which has no parallel in literature, the writers drive on their purpose. "Style," the critic of other centuries talks about. But they did not worry themselves about "style." They did not know they had any style. Purpose? Yes, they had purpose enough. To tell you and me the way in which Christ lived and died; to tell those crazy Galatians that they were false to the whole gospel plan; to tell Israel

* This interchange is admirably illustrated by Mr. Carlyle in his address to the students of Glasgow.

in Babylon that, with determination and spirit, she should be free ; yes, to tell God, in his loving-kindness, that David was abject in penitence. Purpose enough, and that purpose held to, through and through,— held to with such an abandonment of the mere individualism of the writer, that we who read are always tempted to rank Matthew, Mark, Luke, and John all as one, and are almost amazed when some one compels us to notice the distinctions in the way their work is done! But the author keeps himself, almost always, behind his work.

IV. And this impersonality of the authors — their indifference to fame and to criticism — gives only more prominence to the personality, or reference to personal characteristics, which appears all through in the subjects of which they write. Half the later historical books of the Old Testament are the biography of David. The book of Acts lapses, almost by the "law of the instrument," into a biography of Paul. The Gospels make no claim but to be the biography of Christ. These are the great illustrations ; and the rest are, in the same way: "Story of Abraham," "Story of Joseph," "Story of Ruth," "Story of Elijah," "Story of Deborah," "Story of Elijah and Elisha," and the rest. There is none of the ghastliness of our schools of philosophical history. There is a consciousness of the great truth that some man is behind every event in history,— that personal presence and personal power move the world. You may say, indeed, that this is only one illustration more of the necessity for which the Bible exists,— the showing that the Infinite Spirit is the Ruler of finite things. That is true. This illustration, this method in which the personality of the men and women who wrought the marvels is relied upon, is one of the ways in which that truth is forced home upon the world.

My chief effort, then, when I try to explain to young people the best way to read the Bible, is to persuade them to follow out these biographies. They do not like Paul's letters, perhaps. They will come to like them if they will study Paul's biographies, and place the letters, and make real the people to whom he writes. They make nothing of the Old Testament, perhaps. No ? Let them try to make King David stand out on the canvas ; let them find the costume, the scenery and circumstance, of his life ; exult in his exultation when the ark entered conquered Zion, and weep in his agony when Nathan said to him, "Thou art the man." If we once rescue the Bible from that horribly blasphemous habit of reading it by chapter and verse, chopping off one piece for one day and as many inches more for the next day ; if we work out from it, now the life of a conqueror, now the life of a dreamer, now the life of a poet, and, chief of all and first of all, the living life of the Lord of Life, the Saviour of Man, it asserts for us its own moral power, and there is no need of persuasion or of authority to induce us to hold to it from that time forward.

V. For, chiefly, the Bible holds its power over men as the record, in quaint, simple, and unconscious language, of Life and the victories of Life. No literary conceit or pride of authorship, as we saw. No style, long syllables and short syllables, studied metaphor, or other critical or linguistic machinery. Rough style, indeed. You know the Roman Cardinal said he found it bad for his style, so he did not read it. Nay, no great logic ; no system of metaphysic ; no compact method of government ; no treatise on natural history ; no science of morals. Will it tell us whether there is an ocean at the North Pole ? No, it will not tell us that. Will it tell us why God permits evil ? No, it will not tell us that. Will it tell us whether the soul of man existed before he was born into this world ? No. Will it tell us whether the body of man is derived in direct descent from the inferior races ? No. Then what will it tell us ? It will tell us of the power of life ; of the power of God, the Life of the Universe, over all the things which he made and set in order ; of the power of Man, whom God set to subdue the world, to carry out that enterprise when he loyally engages in it ; of the power of the soul, which is the life of man, to control supreme the mind of man, and his body. It tells how the spirit of God moved on the face of the waters. It tells how the inspiration of God led Israel from bondage. It tells how the sense of God lifted Israel from barbarism to command, and how, as Israel lost God, she sank back to vassalage. And such little history is accessory only to the history of histories, the centre of history ; when, in the middle of this book, four untaught men, in narration whose quaint simplicity challenges the criticism and the imitation of the world, describe some incidents in the life of God's own Son, who had no life but God's life, and obeyed no lesser law. In those fragments, there is the triumph of the great Personality of all time. Lord of Life, we call him wisely. And this race of man, which has faith in life, and can have no faith in anything else, this race,— which has always been led and which loves its leaders, which must love them and will love them,— this race of man, which despises abstractions and wants to see the truth,— this race of man, in all its doubts, selfishness, inquiry, is always glad to see the Lord of Life, to hear him speak, and to wonder, and to take to heart his victories. Because the Bible encloses the Four Gospels, explains, illustrates, leads down to them and leads back to them; because, so leading, it shows always that life is always master, and that forms obey,— forms, methods, law, fashion, and all the outside,— that these obey and must obey; because the Bible is the book of Life, and the book of the Lord of Life,— because of this it keeps its hold upon the world.

[This sermon with two sermons on Bible Revision are printed together, in a pamphlet of thirty-six pages, which will be found at the publishers.]

The sermons already published in this series are —

    THE GREAT HARVEST YEAR,
    LOOKING BACK,
    RITUAL,
    PRAYER,
    RESPECTABILITY,
    YOURSELVES,
    WHAT IT IS TO BE CATHOLIC,
    THE JOY OF LIFE,
    THE ASSOCIATED CHARITIES,
    THE REVISION OF THE BIBLE.

They will be sent by mail, in answer to orders addressed to the Publishers, or to R. B. Palfrey, 12 Garland Street, or Box 3196, Boston Post-office. The price of single sermons is ten cents each; for the series of fifteen, the price is one dollar.

12

LENT.

"How turn ye again to the weak and beggarly elements, whereunto ye desire to be in bondage again? Ye observe days and months and times and years. I am afraid of you, lest I have bestowed upon you labor in vain." — GALATIANS iv., 9, 10, 11.

The celebration of Passover was to Israel the celebration of escape from bondage. At the same moment such short winter as Palestine knows comes to an end, and the plains, which will be so arid in midsummer, blush with cyclamens or grow red with anemones. Thus the joyful lesson of spring-time comes in with the lesson of history. It is all one word of gladness. It calls on man, woman, and child to address themselves to life more glad, to thank God for his loving kindness as it appears in awakening life, to rejoice in the blessings with which freedom surrounds them, and to live more than ever to his glory.

There is not a pulpit in Christendom where a preacher might not repeat these remarks, perfectly commonplace as they are, after the 12th of April next. The regulations of the Catholic Church and its imitators will then permit all encouragement and instruction possible to be drawn from lengthening days and the opening spring. According as the moon waxes or wanes at different times, such instructions are proper in Christian pulpits as early as the 23d of March, or as late as the 20th of April. This year happens to be one of the later years, when those Christians, who give in their allegiance to written instructions from mediæval tradition, must postpone to a period well advanced towards our New-England summer, the resolutions and determinations which belong to the new life, new hope, and new joy of longer days of sunshine, and of an unchanging spring.

In place of such exultation, hope, and joy, the Roman Church and its imitators instruct persons who will obey them that the bodies of men,— already more or less impaired in strength and health by the absence of sunlight and the other rigors of winter,— are, in the six weeks of spring-time, to be further reduced, by the use of insufficient food, or food which has not full nourishing power. In place of religious exercises of joy and thanksgiving, she instructs her votaries to join in exercises of penitence and mortification. The line of worship which Syrian idolators adopted to show their grief, and indeed agony,— as the sun declined more and more from day to day,— is the line imposed upon Christian worshippers, by way of showing their halting thanks to God that the decline of the sun is checked, that winter is ended, and that light and life have come. True, this necessity — of reversing every natural lesson of the season — slides backwards and forwards with the moon. The faithful are relieved from it in some years as early as the 3d of March; they are subject to it in others as late as the 20th of April.

Such superstitions need only to be squarely stated to take care of themselves. It needs no argument to show that what is right on the 25th of March in one year cannot well be wrong on another, unless some change have transpired beside the change in the moon's quarterings. Lent, in the original sense of the word, means the lengthening of the days. For us the privilege of Lent is to use the "lenthening." The old New Englanders have not lost the Saxon pronunciation. An old carpenter of the pure blood will tell you — without the letter g — that he is going to "lenthen" the foot-walk, or the shed, or the barn, when the frost is out of the ground. Our duty is to use the freedom in which Jesus Christ has set us free from what Paul calls weak and beggarly elements,— from the observing of days and months and times and years. Our business is to see what are the religious lessons of the emancipation from winter,— what are the pleasures and duties which belong to longer days,— even in a climate like ours, where spring is even more wayward and more coy in her coquetry than belongs to her in the literature of Europe. Of all seasons this has the most distinct religious lessons; for it is a matter of course that a religion whose object is the enlargement of life, will find its most distinct visible lessons in the outside world at the moment when the life of that world is visibly and, in other ways, sensibly renewed.

LENTHEN TIME.

"Soft springing grass, fresh tender flowers,
   The loosened brooks meandering on,
The budding trees and balmy hours,
   Join to proclaim the winter gone.
So, winter of the soul, depart,
   With all your errors, griefs, and fears;
Not this the time to oppress the heart
   With mourning, penance, sighs, and tears.

"Not so had Jesus gladly trod
   The new-born grass of spring renewed;
He looked from Nature up to God,
   And saw the promise always good
Of trust and hope and present love,
   Though dark and rude had winter frowned.
Spring looks not back on clouds and gloom,
   Now 'lenthening days' smile all around." *

It is, indeed, an important thing, in life as artificial as ours, to renew, even by formal acts, the acknowledgment of our relation to what we call outward Nature. We are all linked in with the laws and processes of climate, and, though we pretend to defy them, in our furs, with our fires, and shut up in our houses,— nay, though we pretend to control them, with our batteries, engines, and all the rest of our machinery, — all the same is it true that we are part of the system. We may be masters — yes, but that depends. Now it is an important thing to see that we are masters. We have to study, and, so to speak, to readjust our relation to these laws of Nature. We may not worship the sun, as those wise and shrewd Parsees do to this hour. But, all the same, we have " to see God's beauty in the face of the sun," which is " to see him in the glass of creation." The hardest critic confesses that those men who are at the height of human life — such men as Shakspeare and Spenser and Milton and Goethe, such men as Dante and Homer,— are the men who see Nature best, understand best her symbolism, and know best the hidden life which laughs in her ripples and growls in her tempests. Now we do not ask to be poets, all of us; but we might well ask to be in such sympathy with storm or calm, starlight and sunlight, as the mere right of the sons and daughters of the God who made all these things. It is at a thousand points of the most practical life that this law asserts itself. The doctors will take their patients out-doors at the

* *Old and New*, Vol. I., p. 653.

hospital, to lie on their cots in the sunshine, as soon as the spring grows a little tender, simply that they may bask in the sun's rays. The mother who has any sense puts her puny child by a border in the garden, that she may dig in the earth, and gain fresh strength from her mother, as Antæus did. How often, when you find Rachel weeping for her children, and refusing to be comforted because they are not, do you have to tell her that she must go out every day under the sunshine, or every night under the starlight? From man's poor, broken-down machinery of things and books, with its trail of failures, its measles and diphtherias, its headaches and heartaches, its doubts and its questions, let her go out into God's successful world,— of the snowdrops which never fail, of the stars which no man can explain, of the breezes whose other name is "life," of the sunshine whose other name is "courage." So is it when even successful life, as we choose to call it,— in the successes of society or man's organizations,— becomes too much for us. Your successful merchant, who has made his fortune, finds that the best way to spend it is in trying experiments in agriculture, or other experience which leads him into the open air. All this simulated passion for field sports, which ties feathers and wool into artificial flies, which makes canoes out of pasteboard, and sends young Englishmen to hunt lions in the most sickly climates in the world, is simply the disguised homage which artificial society pays to the native passion for living in the open air. My friend is ashamed to tell me that he is going into the woods from sunrise to sunset to feel God's breezes blow upon him, to see God's sunlight trickle through the leaves, to hear God's birds sing to him, and the very insects hum to him. To do all this for this motive only would be intolerable in our artificial order. But he shows me his patent rod and his patent hooks, his artificial flies and his portable canoe, and he knows that, in the prospect that he will bring home a few little trout, civilized society will justify his enterprise. At the same time he knows, and I know, that what he really prizes is life, simple, lonely, and unfettered,— life in the open air. Indeed, if he and I were by ourselves, not afraid of being thought to talk cant, we should confess to each other that in such escapes he found his nearest communion with God. It is here that belongs Mr. Webster's wise remark that a man can do more work in eight hours than he can in ten, and more in ten months than he can in twelve. Of course he means by the paradox, that if the two extra hours or the two extra months are spent face to face with Nature in the open air, the eight hours and the ten months are of all the more avail.

No man reads the Four Gospels, indeed, with a true sense of their flavor, or, I may say, an adequate comprehension of their language, unless he see how much of that language and the scenery and illustration of the story belongs to open-air life. Shepherds feeding their flocks by night, the weird caravan of astrologers wending their way across the deserts at the bidding of the strange conjunction in the skies,— these are the very beginning of the story. Among the thousands of pictures which the life of Christ has furnished there is not one more suggestive than that in which, under Mary's palm, the heaven-eyed boy sits at midnight on the knees of his mother, who has herself succumbed to sleep, while Joseph, too, is sleeping on the ground; the child, wide-awake and without a thought of earth, looking up at the glories of the infinite stars. Fit illustration of the beginning of the life of him who preaches from the mountain and the deck, on the sea-side, at the lake-side, and in the corn-field, and finds his lessons in lilies and birds' nests, in sunset and in storm. The religious lessons of the Gospels are thus all couched in language which belongs to what people used to be so fond of calling "Natural Theology."

Such justification as the custom of Lent has in Scripture is based, not on the Saviour's words, but on his supposed example. From the most figurative or poetical narrative of his life — the form in which oriental symbolism describes the temptations of personal comfort, of command, and of display — the passage is dissected out which says Christ was forty days in the wilderness, and was an hungered there. For those days he had not had the provision of home and its conveniences. At the end of those days he needed food. On this slender basis is built the extraordinary fabric by which once a year, in the spring-time, the world in its homes, engaged in its daily duties, is told to dispense with its accustomed nourishment. Now if people want to follow literally the Master's habits, they had better do so. If the other part of the narrative were chosen, the change of custom involving change of food and amusement might have its uses. If your high-bred child of civilization, whose every want is anticipated, and his every whim supplied,— if he would go into some wilderness once a year, and see how those people live

who are all needful to him,— it would not be a bad thing for
him. If from the eating and drinking of the club-house, the
carefully-chosen cigars, the favorite wines, the cards and the
billiards, the young American of to-day would go out for six
or eight weeks into the wilderness of America to see how he
can meet its trials and share its hardships,— if there, under
open skies at night, or eating a crust for his dinner at day, he
met the God of the wilderness, and asked him what he was
made for and what he could do,— I can understand that that
fasting, or that "retreat," as the priests would call it, might
be well for him. But if he really mean to follow a Saviour's
personal example, let him follow it. Let us have no poor
travesty of fasting in the midst of our purple and fine linen,
in our houses of cedar and marble.

This eagerness for more out-door life, which comes on us
in the season of lengthening days, belongs, I trust, only to a
larger eagerness,— the eagerness for more life, more chance
to live, and to develop what life we have. Here is the real
and natural side of the instinct, which the Church has got
hold of, and dwarfed and deformed by its mechanism of asceticism. Bees are satisfied to swarm in the spring, birds and
beavers to build, by the law which sets buds to swell and ice
to melt. But man's life — which is of a higher grade and
quality, all through — will never satisfy itself with any material or physical enlargements. Winter or summer, spring or
autumn, man is sure to be seeking more life and more, if he
be a faithful son of an Infinite God. That steady and certain passion will assert itself, when all the things in Nature
are taking new form, by a law perfectly natural. No true
man ever sees the swelling bud, or the forest growing green,
without putting loyally to himself the questions, "And I?"
"How is it with my life?" To take the Testament language
this is the wish for which John Baptist made voice when he
cried, "Make yourself over," "Renew your lives." It is not
the miserable parody of that appeal which the monks and
other preachers have made, which says simply, "Be sorry for
the sins you have committed." It is not repentance merely.
It is renewal. A field which is only sorry for the snow and
ice of winter is a very useless field. It is the other field
green with the rye and oats that snow and ice have nour-
ished, which brings forth fruits fit for repentance. I say the
Mediæval Church took hold of the natural impulse which
every man and woman has in opening spring-time, to be

more manly or more womanly, and travestied it, or loaded it down, with all this mechanism of abstinence and penitence, with these forms of diet and costume, and attendance on visible formulas of worship. But because all that wears out, and cannot stand test, that is no reason why we should refuse attention to the true voice, when we know it is speaking. It is wholly in our power to use Lent, to use these lengthening days, for a real enlargement of our lives; and this means, of course, life on the moral and spiritual side.

1. As all life is knit together into one life — life of the body and life of the mind serving this noble being which a man calls himself — the enlargement of life involves, of course, care for the body and for the mind. Far from cutting off the natural supply of food, it is a man's duty to make sure for himself and his family that their food is nourishing and healthful; that the body may be fully up to any fair requisition which may be put upon it. For the mind — for intellectual power, quickness or soundness of judgment — let a man watch as carefully as he would do in selecting any other tool of his life. As he would choose the best rifle if he were a sportsman, the best axe were he a pioneer, the best saddle if he were going to herd cattle, he chooses whatever discipline or seasoning may give to him the best body or the best mind. If he *have* been living like a hog, if he have been thinking most of the quantity of his food, or if he have chosen his meat for its flavor, or his wines for theirs, of course he renounces such indulgence. If he have been living like a fool, ignorant of the quality of food, or of the laws of digestion and appetite, he sets such folly in order, — chooses his food now by system, eats more if his body need more. He now eats to live; and if he have lived to eat before, he repents of that folly and reforms. In point of fact, though we have, alas! gluttons in our American life, who need to eat less, — and, alas! far too many drunkards who need to drink much less than they do, — the general danger of our habits is the other way. The hurried meal, gorged rather than eaten, which you snatch as you stand, in the fear that you may lose a Western customer, is an offence to the laws of health — which are laws of God — as insulting as is any debauch or gluttony. You know better than I, whether it do not speak selfishness and carelessness of eternal laws as truly. For the sex of women, the general verdict of those medical men who have most studied the nervous diseases of American women is, that they do not eat enough.

"All American women are under-fed," says Dr. William Hammond, boldly; and he is one of the highest authorities. It is not my duty here to discuss this dictum, or to impress it, but it is worth repeating in the connection which we are tracing. Here is a very simple illustration of the folly of letting the Greek bishops of the third century adjust the fashions of religious observance of American women in the nineteenth. Enough is it for man or woman to select and use the food and the drink which shall give the tools most useful to the commanding soul.

2. The man who would enlarge his life, will, of course, go much farther than the mere schooling of his mind or the mere discipline of his body. "Men talk to me of faith," such a man will say; "Have I, or have I not, used to the best the institutions of worship? Have I, or have I not, sought fairly and unselfishly the company and sympathy of my fellow-men in the offices of worship?" And an honest man will be apt to own that he does not try to live alone in anything else. In politics he is one of the Commonwealth; in business he is related to his fellows in partnerships, in corporations and companies, in syndicates and boards; in amusement he never tries to be alone, not for half an hour; in society he is always seeking clubs and other parties. As an honest man, he will say that, for his religious life, he ought to associate with other men. In enlarging life he will say that he ought to join with others in worship. If he have neglected his church-going his resolutions of enlarging life will make him more careful. To praise God with his fellow-men; with them to join in prayer; with them, were it merely in entering church together, to acknowledge weakness and the need of strength,— to do this is a part of what he needs for life more abundant.

3. An honest man will say again, "Am I thinking of myself too much,— for a man who wants more life?" And an honest man who is not a fool will know that life shrinks away and is shrivelled to nothing when a man does live for himself alone. "Have I, perhaps, neglected my family," he asks himself, "in this eager care that when I am dead they may inherit a competency?" Can a man do better for his children than to be sure that they love him? Can children inherit a better patrimony than those children have who have a loving father, whose life quickens theirs, and who is their best playmate in childhood, and in youth their best friend? "Because I wish for a larger life," such a man

says in his Lenten repentances, "I will live more with my family, I will be more at home."

4. "My life is to be larger," he says again. And he may find out that it is narrow in this, that when his neighbors are at work for the city, for the State, for the fisheries, for the art museum, for the poor, for the orphans, for the hospitals, or for the heathen, he is at work for nobody. He is quite sure, he says, that the relief of the poor makes more beggars than it saves. He is quite sure, he says, that the brats saved to life by the Sea Shore Home might better die. He is quite sure that the rivalry between two or three hospitals is folly. All doctors are humbugs, he says, and one as much as another. Easy, my friend, to find such reasons why you will not join in this or that cause which interests your neighbor. But if you want a larger life than you have, you must find some cause, somewhere, where your heart shall beat and your wit devise for other men. We will not urge you to take up one of these humbugs or follies which your wit derides, or your wisdom strips so bare. But some field you must find, outside your own selfishness, for your charge, or you can have no knowledge what life abundant is.

5. "If I would enlarge my life," a thoughtful man says, "I must enlarge the circle of my companions." And, because a man now finds most of his companions in his reading, he asks who are his daily companions. If he find that most of his reading has been supplied to him by a telegraph operator in Bulgaria, a special correspondent in Afghanistan, a police reporter in New York, or some unknown traveller in Southern Africa,— that is to say, if he find that in confining his reading to the newspapers he is confining his company to a circle of anonymous people whom he never saw nor heard of,— he determines to take a step out, and to enlarge his company. He can introduce into his parlor the noblest men and women of this time or of any time. He has only to resolve, and the barrier of language melts away. The wits of France, the wise men of Germany, then men of practice of England, accept his invitations as he chooses, and stay till he dismisses them. In the choice of such society is a steady enlargement of life.

6. And then this question comes to him soon, "How much am I with the Leader of Life,— how well do I know him,— how much do I listen to him?" For, as we live, a man's knowledge of Jesus Christ, the Saviour of the world, may be the merest outside respect, paid somewhat as a French flower-girl might think of the statue of King Dagobert above her as she

sells her wares,—some very great king, of whom she knows nothing. "How well do I know the Leader of Life,—the Saviour of this world?" A man who really means to enlarge his life asks that question only to answer it man-fashion. He will not be satisfied with remembering a parable or two, or a scrap here and there from talk or sermon. He makes the Four Gospels a study, and he finds that the books which illustrate them open right and left into all history, and throw on Christ's career such light as to make him intelligible, and a real being in human affairs. To such a determination — to choose as a personal friend the Master of Life — the answer may be slow, but it is sure. Let the man who makes that choice set apart his seasons and occasions for entering into the society of Jesus Christ. Let him put himself in the place of apostles, of men of the multitude, of listeners by the lake-side, and he shall find, year in and year out, that more and more surely Jesus Christ comes to him as a present leader and firm friend, and in trial, in anxiety or in joy, and in eventful living, is his present saviour here and now.

7. Yes; and let a man be sure to select the highest company of all, if he would truly live. I am not alone, he says, for the Father is with me. I walk under the stars, and I am with the God who sets them in order. I lie awake at night,—here is God with me, in whose law my heart is beating. Father, give life to thy child. Inevitably and surely the answer comes, "Son, I am ever with thee, and all that I have is thine." For this Infinite Power — the Conscious Life of the Universe, whose best name is Father — is willing to give his strength for my weakness, and to lift me to be fellow-workman in his designs. If I really seek to enlarge my life, I may enlarge it, not in any human measurements, but by the Infinite proportions.

The sermons already published in this series are —

>THE GREAT HARVEST YEAR,
>LOOKING BACK,
>RITUAL,
>PRAYER,
>RESPECTABILITY,
>YOURSELVES,
>WHAT IT IS TO BE CATHOLIC,
>THE JOY OF LIFE,
>THE ASSOCIATED CHARITIES,
>THE REVISION OF THE BIBLE,
>THE BIBLE.

They will be sent by mail, in answer to orders addressed to the Publishers, or to R. B. Palfrey, 12 Garland Street, or Box 3196, Boston Post-office. The price of single sermons is ten cents each; for the series of fifteen, the price is one dollar.

13

NEW LIFE.

John the Baptist came preaching and saying, Repent ye, for the kingdom of heaven is at hand.— MATT. iii., 1, 2.

The appeal is the appeal for a New Life,— life on a higher plane. It is not a mere demand for sorrow for the past : it is a demand that the future shall be all different from the past. Nor is the difference a difference of method simply ; it is difference of quality. The old existence may have been functional, mechanical, and formal. The new existence is to be vital, spontaneous, and original. Man is to change from being a beast. He is to live. He is to be a child of God.

The critics are fond of dwelling on the fact, that this is better expressed in the Greek than it is in our English. This is true. The original implies new thought,— what we call reflection, a turning back only that one may go forward. And the analogy of all that John Baptist said, and the Saviour as well, shows that this is no mere verbal comment, but is the key and clue to the whole gospel lesson. Thus, the moment Christ comes face to face with the learning of his country as represented by Nicodemus, all he has to tell him is that he must be renewed. The lesson is the simple lesson of the three other Gospels : that a man must become "as a little child"; must start on his new life with as much vitality as has a healthy child new-born ; must grow as fast, and be, from time to time, as conscious of advancing. At which the mechanical people in the world look, wondering,— and they listen as well as wonder,— and say, "Where, Lord, and how?" "In what modes shall we grow, and in what forms encase ourselves?" An appeal this at which Jesus fairly laughs, and so do all who have his spirit. For the exact character of the New Life is that it defies form, and just what he and John the Baptist are insisting on is, that people shall lead a new life, and not try to reproduce an old one. They are to live by the Spirit, and the Spirit will make the form.

I had occasion to speak at the "Teachers' Club," on Tuesday, of the great evil that for centuries on centuries has, to half the Christian world,— and more than half at times,— transformed this great word, "Renew Yourself," involving this great duty always fresh and new. The word has been so twisted round that, in Latin or in other languages, all Catholics read, "Do Penance," instead of "Renew Yourselves." Now, if anything can be different from what John Baptist and Jesus Christ meant, it is doing penance in the modern notion. And it is hard to conceive of any accident of language which should have brought in so much contradiction and falsehood, as this single case of falling away from a demand so overwhelming. What these leaders of life propose is new life inspired by a higher spirit. They exhaust language to show that it is to be life indeed, rather than any wretched imitation. What is granted them, on the other hand, in the "doing of penance," is a set of observances, mechanical of their very nature, very likely prescribed by code, and, at the worst, suggesting that *things* have a value of their own. Nothing can so confuse the penitent, and nothing can so thwart the purpose of the Saviour.

I. A new quality of life. That is the demand of Christianity, and that is what it obtains in its real victories. All the time it is true, that you may have a form of life which in the externals looks so like the real article, that no one can tell which is which till it is tried. So I may go to the cutler's shop, and have two knives placed before me, of which one is as beautiful as the other, handle, shank, and blade. My eye discovers no difference. But, in truth, one is of iron untempered, and the edge will give way at the first blow; the other is of steel of such temper that it fairly seems to improve by use. The simile may be pressed a little farther. For the maker of steel has processes by which he will take an iron plate, or an iron knife, or even a pair of iron scissors, and will subject them to a treatment which, it must be confessed, involves a good deal of heating, and perhaps some sudden chills, but from the end of which the tool or the plate comes out high-tempered steel. So it is with God's processes. The man may go into the furnace good for nothing, soft of texture, unfit for use. He shall come out of that furnace fit for life eternal; yes, even with the polish that endures, and with the grit and edge that deal with the eternal necessities. All this, however, involves and demands a wholly new quality in the man. That quality, Saint Paul calls the Divine Spirit or the "Holy Spirit." To receive that new life is to be born again.

And let me say, in passing, that, though the world is forever trying to invent some outside marks — one almost calls them trade-marks — by which he who has life of the higher quality may be distinguished from him who has it not, the world never succeeds. From the nature of the case, it must fail. It is as easy to put "Rogers, Sheffield, best steel," on the iron carving-knife as it is upon that which is most prudently and wisely tempered. I am not sure but it is easier. And it is as easy for the carnal brute, just wakened from yesterday's headache, hating the liquor which brought it on and the man who supplied it, — it is as easy for him to "do penance," in some outward service of penance, as it is for the saint nearest God and most alive with his life. But, in the one case, the rainbow of promise lasts only as long as the cloud on which it is painted. The repentance and the penance may last no longer than the nausea and the headache. As John Baptist knew, and as Jesus Christ always said, "The tree must be known by its fruits,"—and the man. No zinc label wired on the branches, no title on the nurseryman's catalogue, no color of the bark, no beauty of the blossom, will suffice. Good fruit, good tree. Bad fruit, bad tree. No fruit, and there might as well be no tree. Good cutting, good knife. Bad cutting, bad knife. No cutting, and there might as well be no knife. Good work, good man. Bad work, bad man. No work, and there might as well be no man.

II. I have, however, very little to do with this substitution for renewal of doing penance,— the device, not unnatural, of a church whose life was dying out of it. That is not our danger here. There is no danger that any of us will be fasting, or going to church six times in a week, or bearing any other such physical burden, by way of doing penance for our sins. No. The danger with us is what the danger was to soldiers to whom John Baptist preached,— to publicans who came to consult him,— to city gentlemen who, to their own surprise, were waked up by news of the prophet, so that they took horse for a twenty-mile ride out of Jerusalem into the country, and asked John what they should do. He would tell us just what he told them. He told them that they were all in the ruts; that they did what they did, not because they wanted to do it, or cared anything about the principle of it, but because other people had done it. They did it because it was the fashion, or the old custom, or because it was easy; in brief, because it was "the way" agreed upon. And he told them to wake up, and to do what they did, henceforth, with thought and spirit; to do it with the fresh life of sons and daughters of God. "God is here," he said; "use the present spirit. Renew your whole way of life, for your Father, God, is here at hand!" If he had a chance, he would say the same thing to us to-day. You observe that he did not tell the soldier that he must quit soldiering and take to the work of relieving poor people. That is a modern blunder. The soldier is to go on with his soldiering,— though soldiering under Herod or Pilate must have had its drawbacks. But he is to do it rightly, and not wrongly. He is to do it with a conscience, and not as a machine. "Do violence to no one," says the Baptist, with a certain grim humor, when speaking to the roistering bully of the garrison, "and be content with your wages." The publican is to be a publican still, hateful though that business were to all the people who paid taxes. There is an honorable way to collect taxes also, and a son of the present God need not be ashamed to be in that calling. Only let him do his work, as God does his,— "Exact no more than is appointed you." In our lives, it does not require much imagination to apply the lesson. Thus, Thomas or Harry is called to-day by his master, and bidden just at nightfall to take a letter down town to the general post-office to save the evening mail. The young man is enraged that a moment's forgetfulness of his master should exact of him an hour's journey, just to repair that minute's failure. He takes the letter and goes and returns, grumbling all the way that fate has made him a slave to such a tyrant. The next day, the woman whom he worships with a secret love asks him if he can make a chance to take her letter to the post? She does not dare trust it to the pillar-box. It is the first favor she ever asked of him. To render her the humblest service is a victory. The young fellow walks on air as he goes through the same streets in which, the day before, he was cursing himself as a slave. The thing done is the same thing. Yes, to the eye. But it is done with a life all new and changed. That little illustration will help us, if it show us that the gift of Life proposed to us is not, in the outset, any change of place, of service, or of any outward duty. But it does propose an infinite enlargement of the motive power by which duty is performed.

The Chinese painter in his workshop at Canton is told to copy a portrait of Washington. He does as he is told. Stroke by stroke, line by line, he imitates the pattern set before him. He would do as well, he would do as ill, were he copying Paul Potter's famous bull, or were he copying the curves, without meaning, of a veneer of maple wood. The picture is worthless when it is finished. On the other hand, Gilbert Stuart, or Felix Darley, or William Hunt is asked to do his best to make one more picture of Washington. It may be the roughest sketch,— there may be not fifty strokes upon the canvas; but it is alive with all the enthusiasm and gratitude which the artist felt for the hero whom he loved. As the marble-worker in an Italian studio, filing down the surface of a Hebe or a Diana, measuring every line, smoothing just so far and no farther, just as the rule may direct,— as he differs from the sculptor himself, pursuing always the flying, dreamy figure which his mind sees, and trying to reproduce that in the stone,— so does that man's life which is mere routine and imitation differ from the life of him who has an idea of love, and truth, and purity, which quickens every deed of to-day, though it be the buckling of his shoe or the sweeping of a floor. The captious critic looked at Michael Angelo's bronze horses, and pointed out endless mistakes in the anatomy. "But alas!" he said; "for all this the cursed brutes are alive."

Now Jesus Christ's purpose and determination is, that we shall live, even in every day's routine and mechanism. Are we machines, are we mere animals when he finds us,— Nathanael in his garden, John and Andrew at their fish-net, Mary Magdalene in her home of seven temptations, Matthew at that tax-gatherer's bureau? He does not mean to leave us machines. No more routine life! No more mere animal being! "The kingdom of God is within you." Within you! That is nigh indeed. "Men shall not say lo here, or lo there." I need not go to hear Chrysostom preach. I need not study law or prophets, to learn what are the modes of my duty. I need not tell forty beads to-day and forty-two to-morrow. I need not sing this hymn, nor phrase that prayer. For the kingdom of God is within me. God is willing to make me his ally. The Father's life quickens me,— yes, for these duties next my hand,— because I am his child.

Let me, then, accustom myself to the study of the infinite relations of my daily duty. Thus, to hoe the ground here, and soften it; to break my back as I stoop to cut up these potatoes, and then to count out so many eyes — no more and no less — to each hill; this is not agreeable nor easy. No. Nobody ever said it was. But many a man has learned to carry on such work as that, not as a beast which drudges, but as a child of God who must be about his Father's business.

"I say I love these children of mine: shall I pretend to love them, and not be willing to spend and be spent that they may be fed? Or shall I pray to God for my daily bread, and not be willing to do my share in this garden, which is a little share in the infinite circuit in which the sun in the heavens, the winds as they blow, the night as it cools the dews, answer that prayer up to the very edge of its accomplishment, only leaving to me the privilege, as of an archangel, of giving that last touch which completes the whole?"

"Or, I call myself one of the great family of mankind; and I am. Am I, then, such a shirk and sneak that, while sailors are sailing for me, soldiers fighting for me, planters planting for me, spinners spinning for me, weavers weaving for me, miners mining for me, and smiths forging for me, I — fine gentleman that I am — say rather palsied idiot — I am to lie here on a bank of sod and do nothing for them? Better lie five feet beneath it!"

These are, I know, only clumsy formulas for the way in which brave men address themselves to repulsive duties. But there is this power innate in man,— and it is this which Jesus Christ insists upon,— by which a brave man lifts himself above the earth, or is lifted by the Spirit of God within him. It makes "humble labors shine," as God makes them noble, or, as the catechism says so well, " as man lives to God's glory."

I am fond of watching men as I see them return in the evening from their daily duty,— to guess with which of them it has been cheerful work, and with which of them it has been grinding labor. For this is to say, which of them carried God with him, that morning, to be his helpmeet in what the day demanded, and which of them chose to go alone. That man has debased himself to the drudgery, meaner than slavery, of a senseless battery,— so much acid here, and so much zinc there; a little bread, a little meat, and a little water, changed into human muscle, and then, by that dead drudgery, changed back again into carbon and nitrogen. It is the difference between the two women who were grinding in the same mill : one of them is taken, and one, as the Bible says so grimly, is left. One is taken into absolute, glad communion with the infinite God, and the other is left grovelling and groping among mills and millstones, chaff and dirt, and other perishable things of time. Such is the difference between the man who is renewed, reformed, waked up, so as to live with God's Spirit, as the partner of his love, and that other wretch, whom I might not strictly call a man, who has chattered out his poor protest, " How can I be born when I am old ? " He has been content to drudge on, uninspired, in the old routine, without heart, because without life, and only repeating, as a dead pebble repeats, the clatter and rumble of all the pebbles that have been driven up and down stupidly by the tides before.

III. "Brace up,— this is God's world." Into some such language would young America to-day put the great injunction, in its fear of Scriptural language, or its gradual disuse of it. Clear enough it is, that any man who really knows his own relationship to the God of the universe cannot be depressed by the doubts of the man who is trying to work along alone, as if he, poor little atom, were floating free in these oceans of time and space, with nobody to help him, or nobody even to care for him. To that terror no man can sink who knows he is God's child, and that God is here,— a conscious, present power. But one must know this, and keep it in mind. The direction is not simply that a man renew himself, reform himself, repent and turn round,— or, in that phrase of modern slang, that he "brace up" anew,— but it supplies the reason : " Repent, for the kingdom of God is at hand." Three things let a man see and know and feel : First, that he is not an atom, but that he is in some sort of kingdom or commonwealth. Second, that this organism of which he is — this commonwealth or kingdom — is God's kingdom. And this is not enough. Third, let him know and feel also that God's kingdom is not a hard, foreordained, and cruel empire, depending on some deaf and dumb law, arranged no one knows how, why, or when; but that it is the present rule of the present love of a present Father, who is here and now. This is to know, in Christ's phrase, that the " kingdom is at hand."

1. First, let me get well beyond that separate or lonely notion of the atoms, be it haughtiness or be it humility. Let me find out, by experiment, if I can find it out in no other way, what it is to live in the common life,— helping and helped, giving and taking. I say, learn it by experiment if in no other way. For I think no man has fairly tried the experiment but is sure that it succeeds. No man has loyally met his brother-man more than half-way — has fairly stepped out of his shyness or his crustiness, to lend a hand and to take a hand — but, in the long run, is glad he has done it. No man ever really put his head out of his snail-shell, to see if there were an outside world, and if there were social life, but he liked the outlook so well — God's heavens, man's society, and woman's love — that he never fell back forever on snail-shell life again. Fairly try mutual life, the life in common, and you will know that you are not meant to be alone; you are a member of a great kingdom to which you can give, and from which you must receive.

2. What Jesus Christ tells you next — and this, too, you can confirm by experiment if you will — is, that this is God's kingdom, and not the devil's kingdom; no, nor man's kingdom. It is a kingdom where right rules in the long run, and where, in the long run, crime is powerless and sin a failure. Its laws are eternal laws, and they are laws which all work in together; so that the fisherman who rightly cures his fish in the mouth of the St. Lawrence, the Indian woman who rightly prepares for the hunting in Alaska, the boy who rightly draws the furrow by the Red River, and the man who rightly adds up columns in a day-book in Franklin Street are all at work together, in a mutual order, devised and ordered for the good of the whole world. Right work of any man tells for the good of the whole. This means that the whole is ruled for good and by good, or that it is God's kingdom.

3. And this kingdom, in which the Sons and Daughters of God have their posts of duty assigned to them now, is at hand. We are of it, are in it; nay, have much of its pomp and etiquette and law to administer. Our King has not forgotten us, to go and see after some distant Sirius, or some rebellious comet which is trying to escape him. Our King is the Father of his people. He goes and comes among us,— happy that we are happy, caring for our cares, and determined to help us through. At our tables, lo, the King! In our amusements, lo, the King! In our doubts, here is the Father! In our grief,— nay, at an open grave,— the Father

is caring for his child! The Saviour who begs you to renew your life, and to live on the plane on which God's angels live, tempts you to do so, by saying that this tender kingdom of a Father's thoughtful love is always here, at hand.

Nor does he leave this to his statement, or to the Baptist's. We have all seen those statements verified a thousand times. You and I have seen those of God's children who are the least favored in worldly favor, who yet enjoy his own control of the things around, and make this world a part of heaven, in loyalty to him, and in the real communion. I have seen a sewing-girl come home from her ten hours' task to the care of her crippled mother, to find that home a paradise, because both daughter and mother shared it with the Unseen Father. It is his home while it is theirs. His infinite love is there. His abundant life is there. The flowers,— no, they were not cut in a greenhouse; they are the simple geraniums and the cacalias, the Wandering Jew and the tiarella, which the window sun is sufficient for. But they are alive,— alive with the Father's life, with the mother's care, and with the girl's delight. For that delight has the mother cared for them and tended them. The books,— no, they are not gorgeous in binding, nor gilt upon the edges. They have the sordid covers of the public library use, and they will be sent back to-morrow to take turn in cheering another home. But the pretty book-mark between the pages — which is token of the daughter's love for her mother — is only one visible sign of the tenderness which has given to the poet's verse more sweetness, to the novelist's passion more ardor, or to the philosopher's epigram more meaning, as through the happy evening the daughter reads to her half-blind mother. The furniture,— no, it is not of the Renaissance, nor of the second empire, nor of any school or design but the school of frugality tempered by love. But the chair-tidy yonder was a Christmas present from a shop-mate; the cushion behind her back was the handiwork of the girl who tends in the cigar-shop down stairs; the foot-rest in front of the fire was carved by that German boy who runs the errands at the store. There is hardly a piece of the *bizarre* collection but, as the angels read, is written all over with the legends that tell of brotherly or sisterly love, or the love of child or of mother. That is the reason why this home is paradise. It is in such fashion that the kingdom of God is visibly at hand; for the God of love lives in that little household, as certainly as on any heights of Zion, or in any cold courts of constellations or stars, or "interstellar spaces." When the loving mother and the loving daughter meet again in that cheerful home, after one has finished her day of loneliness and the other her day of work, there is the present kingdom, and there the God whose name is Father.

Make your lives over, saith the Saviour ; live on the higher plane of love and faith and hope : for this kingdom of certain power and of certain joy is at hand,— at every man's hand. It is life with all who live, the triumph and blessedness of him who knows that the great family of mankind thus presses forward together, under one lead, to one victory. It is life with the living God, the triumph and blessedness of him who knows that God helps out his endeavors, that God lifts him when he falls, that God prompts him when he forgets, that God teaches him if he is ignorant, that God gives him life when he faints, that God gives him strength when he is weary. That child of God tries the promise, and lo the sway and empire of God are at hand !

14

Blasphemy against the Holy Ghost.

Glad tidings of great joy, which shall be to all people. — LUKE ii., 10.

"Tell me God loves me." This was the appeal to me once of a woman who had borne every form of suffering, and had so found the Divine strength that she bore it well. "When we come to church," she said, "we people who have to bury in the ground our dearest, who have to live under the tyranny of custom, and are chained to the wheels of ten thousand follies,— we who nurse drunken fathers, and bear the stripes, worse than blows, of bitter words,— we come to church that you may tell us *God loves us*. I know he loves me," she said bravely, "but I want you to tell me so again."

This is an expression, in the language of our time, of the spirit in which the real disciples received Jesus Christ, and the spirit in which he wanted them to receive him. To speak simply, he opposed himself to the whole notion of terror. Men are not to fear God any longer. These tidings of his are Good Tidings. That is to say, Jesus squarely opposes himself to every form of Heathenism, Devil-worship, Pharisaism, Manicheism, or Calvinism — which would make out God a cruel God. To all that whine, which we hear now and then, that Nature is cruel, he firmly says, "No." The Gospel, the Good Word, the Glad Tidings, are the announcement of the unity of nature between us and God. His life is ours, ours is his. There is no jar to be reconciled, no break to be mended. Our lives are hid in him. And his spirit inspires us, unless we shut the doors and keep it out.

Every now and then, the Christian religion seems to take a new start in the world. It takes on perhaps a new ritual. A new set of prophets take up the work which dozing priests have dropped from their hands. It seems to need a new name, so different are its glad voices from the groans of years before. These fresh starts are always due to the new announcement of "glad tidings." Religion means love again. Deviltry and vengeance and cruelty are trodden under the feet of the reformers who lead in the Saviour in these times. Yet, again, the message is this simple message which it was in the beginning,— that God loves us all.

Take it, however, in Christ's own time :— these common people who heard him gladly, these sinners whom he made so welcome, this Mary Magdalene from whom he drove her seven devils, all start up in joy, as the lark starts when he welcomes sunrise. God has been to them a Judge to be bribed; God is a Father who loves them. Religion has been the killing of doves and sheep and oxen on an altar; religion is — why, it is the child's sinking to rest in his father's arms, murmuring out a child's love, while it hears a full assurance of a father's.

You can catch just a glimpse of the same thing in the salutations at the end of Paul's epistles. What made religion run so like wildfire in those low-toned Greek cities, and in the very slums of Rome? Why, because religion is "glad tidings" to this lonely shopkeeper; to that abused freedman; to the slave who is whipped every day by the chief of the servants; to the widow whose son was killed yesterday in the amphitheatre. It is glad tidings to those who sit in the shadow of death.

It is the same thing when Luther starts the whole world of the north into new life which it has never lost. The Pope Leo is frightening them with his hells,— is asking them to buy themselves free by this and that tribute; and Luther cries, "You *are* free if you only trust God," and they fling off the chains of centuries, and exult in the gladness of freemen.

Fifty years after, there went down into Hungary a man who did not know their language well, but who, in such language as he had, appealed not to princes or priests, but to the people. They heard him preach with a perfect frenzy. There was no cathedral so well fortified but they flung its gates open, that this preacher of the people might preach his gospel there. He changed the whole form of the religion of that land; and he did this by no magic but the simple magic of this simple gospel of a loving God. Thus was it that Hungary became Unitarian. And that is the story of the way in which Methodism swept England and America. It was the opening up, even to poor wretches in the dark shafts of mines and coal-pits, of the infinite meaning of that word "salvation." Treasures were in their hands such as princes and kings might envy; and these treasures are not to be bought or slaved for, but this is a free salvation.

And, on the other hand, whenever the miracle stops, or seems to stop, it is because some set of dried-up, purblind priests have come to be fumbling over some formalism of doctrine or ritual, and have even made that system to be stupid and hard and cruel and dead, which was, is, and ought to be the religion of "glad tidings," the love of God and the love of man.

In the midst of this treasure-house of the blessings thus given to mankind, there are — oh, the pity that it is so! — just two or three dark texts in Scripture, which seem to point another way. And among the purblind priests, and among the faint-hearted complainers, of whom there must be some in a world not yet perfect, there are always just enough people to exaggerate and harp upon these two or three words of mystery. What is much worse, in the dark ages of any kind, in the countries and times when ignorance and disease and sin, and what I called "deviltry" in general, have had their way, the discouraged men, the sick men, and the wicked men have had too much share in coloring literature and language with bloody stains, for which these two or three texts gave the excuse. And these are the reasons why these two or three dark texts which, at the first glance, can be made to imply cruelty or something akin to it on the part of God, are dwelt upon, yes even in hymns and in sermons, more than are a thousand of the proclamations of good-cheer and joy.

Here is the reason why, in the ebb years, as I may call them, in the periods when the world and the Church settle back from one of the epochs of Christian victory, Religion girds herself with that scowl and frown which become her typical costume. Here is the reason why religious people are thought to be out of place in places of joy or amusement, and the exercises of religion to be as dull as they are solemn. But these reasons cannot go back to the joyous journey of the Saviour through Galilee, nor to the memory of the days when men ridiculed him because he came eating and drinking, and when they reviled his followers because they did not fast. They belong, and the sanctions for them belong, only to dark ages, to the heathenism which surrounded Christianity in its cradle, and to the ignorance and disease which it has not wholly conquered now.

Let me speak of one of these texts for a moment, because I have been asked by an inquirer I do not know, on the other side of the world, to give my view of it. It is the text which has to answer for, I dare not say how much, insanity, and for how much of that gloom which is close akin to insanity. It is the text which, as we read, says that "he who blasphemes the Holy Ghost shall not be forgiven, neither in this world nor in the world to come." Some discouraged soul sinks into the notion that he has blasphemed the Holy Ghost, and thenceforth forever is an outcast in God's universe. As one of these meteors astray in space seems to know no resting-place, no companionship, nothing but the white glare of the unfriendly sun, so such a soul persuades himself that he is without forgiveness, without home, and away from God. And, what is worse, this sentence is supposed to be inflicted as a part of the gospel, or "glad tidings."

Now, all this is only the interpretation which dark ages give to one of the commonplaces of human expression. Grant the monkish pictures of hell, grant the notion of God sitting as a judge, the Holy Ghost sitting over against him as another God, and souls brought up one by one for trial, as in the famous Egyptian pictures, or in Michel Angelo's, more famous, and you see how this color is given to these words. But dismiss all that imagery as so much heathenism, come back to the Saviour's own language, and listen to his own words, and you find serious expostulation — yes — with these so willing to make him a devil, but never his denunciation of unending woe.

What is forgiveness?

Let us distinguish between the reality and the symbol of it.

A boy commits an offence at school, or many offences. He has on the record such marks to show his bad conduct that he is to be punished. Then he tells his master that he is sorry. He is sorry. The marks are rubbed out, and the punishment is omitted. Now, the forgiveness there is matter between the boy and his master. Confidence begins between them again. The master believes the boy, the boy promises the master. But the *sign* of forgiveness is a wholly different matter, not to be confounded with the reality.

Or a man steals a loaf of bread from a window. He is sent to prison. In prison his keepers are satisfied that he is sorry, and will not offend so again. The Governor is satisfied that he has been punished sufficiently. The Governor, as the spokesman for the Commonwealth, forgives his offence against the State, pardons him, and unlocks the prison door. The forgiveness is in the mutual confidence restored between the stronger and weaker party. The opening the prison is only the *sign* of this forgiveness.

So when a child rebels against God, fights against him. His forgiveness comes when the fight is over; when he takes God's law for his law, and they two are at one. The signs of forgiveness are many, but they are nothing unless this real reconciliation of the child's stubborn nature have come first.

Now when such a Saviour as Jesus Christ speaks of forgiveness, he speaks of this return of God's child to his allegiance to God. The child is tired of rebellion, and, like the prodigal, comes home. He is forgiven. He is at one with God again. But the Church of the Middle Ages,— oh, the pity!— when it spoke of forgiveness meant only the symbol or sign of such reunion. God was a judge, and forgiveness meant unbolting the cell, and meant nothing more. Or, God was a king, and forgiveness meant striking off the chains, and nothing more. An escape from hell was forgiveness. A cooling of the flames of hell was forgiveness. But this has really nothing to do with the Saviour's notion of "forgive" and "forgiveness." Forgiveness, as he speaks, is the loosening of sin, the silencing of passion, and the return of the alienated child to God.

Thus he says, "Whosesoever sins ye loosen, they are loosened." The real apostle has power to loosen and make weaker the temptations of men, till they become nothing. And in this passage, he says the temptation and the power of sin over men will be loosened,— made less and less. Such is, indeed, the whole object of his life. Nor is he troubled about men's abuse of him. Let them abuse him. That sin also will be loosened,— it will not hold them always. But while a Pharisee or scribe or anybody is resisting the power of God in his own heart, he is putting off the very help by which passion is to be tamed and sin loosened. Man or angel, while defying God, cannot be helped by God. And if either man or angel need God's help, the condition is the simple condition of ceasing from rebellion, or from what is here called "blasphemy." Let man cease,— or angel,— and the remission of sin begins,— its loosening,— what our Bibles call its "forgiveness." Angel and God are one again; man and God are one again. But while man turns his back to God, he will not see God's face. And while he talks of

Satan and Beelzebub and all evil spirits as taking the work and place of God himself, while he makes them gods in place of the Infinite and Holy Spirit, he cannot find himself inspirited by that Spirit, or living in the Infinite Life.

Trust God, if you would have infinite strength. This is the lesson. Neither angel nor man can have the strength which is infinite while he relies on his own.

But suppose you take the language of the Saviour,— strong but not vindictive,— and set the fancy of the Middle Ages at work upon it. In place of forgiveness or the loosening of sin, substitute the release from some punishment of sin. In place of the love of the Father,— all-embracing, all-subduing,— substitute this mythical Third Person, sitting in human form upon his throne in the heavens. Picture then this offending rebel hurling his insult on his inhuman sovereign. Picture God the Father sending his archangels to seize the wretch, and to cast him, for that act of insult, into unending torture. There you have the heathenish conceit which has been imposed upon the framework of a gospel which deserves no such travesty.

Shut your eyes to that picture, if you are weary and heavy laden. Turn away as well from the rattle and noise of a world which, when it is least successful, is most noisy. And when all else is still, listen again to a Saviour's simple word of courage. Call it commonplace if you will,— so much the better for people who are commonplace, like you and me. Do not trust in your own perseverance, he says. Do not trust in your own experience. Do not trust in your own strength. Build on the rock, and not on the sand. Take God's strength for your strength, God's wisdom for your wisdom, God's life for your life.

Then, he says, these temptations of earth shall be less and less. This power of sin shall be steadily loosened.

While you oppose him, and would fain set your passion against his purpose, you cannot escape the penalty of passion. Not if you were an archangel in the other world.

But when you seek him, surely you shall find him. In this world or in that world, he is ready for his children. And lo, you have the power which rules the universe to still your passions, and to remit your sins.

The sermons already published in this series are —

> THE GREAT HARVEST YEAR,
> LOOKING BACK,
> RITUAL,
> PRAYER,
> RESPECTABILITY,
> YOURSELVES,
> WHAT IT IS TO BE CATHOLIC,
> THE JOY OF LIFE,
> THE ASSOCIATED CHARITIES,
> THE REVISION OF THE BIBLE,
> THE BIBLE,
> LENT,
> NEW LIFE.

They will be sent by mail, in answer to orders addressed to the Publishers, or to R. B. Palfrey, 12 Garland Street, or Box 3196, Boston Post-office. The price of single sermons is ten cents each; for the series of fifteen, the price is one dollar.

THE FUTURE OF NEW ENGLAND.

In speaking of the future of New England, I am following in the steps of Dr. Ezra Stiles, as he addressed a convention on the same subject, one hundred and nineteen years ago. He was one of the most careful scholars of New England in the period just before the American Revolution. His studies on various subjects are well worth our attention now; and of all his published works, none is more interesting than his discourse "On the Christian Union," delivered in Bristol, Rhode Island, April 23, 1760.

In this discourse, he goes into very careful statistics, to show what will be the probable increase of New England, first in the next century, and then in several hundred years after, till the millennium. Without following the detail, which shows care and judgment unusual among men who forecast the future, I will say simply that his prophecy is, that in the year 1860 the population of Connecticut, Rhode Island, and Massachusetts would be about eight millions of people. He makes allowance for the considerable settlement of Vermont; he takes notice of the fact that Nova Scotia is already receiving settlers from New England; and with a certain generosity, quite striking in the praise of his own home, he says: "If Providence shall complete the reduction of Canada and an honorable peace to the British Crown, we may extend our settlements to new provinces, or to the western parts of those provinces which, by their charters, cross the continent to the Pacific Ocean." But he does not anticipate any such settlement on a very large scale. He says "the present bounds of New England, the greater part of which is a wilderness, permit an increase of seven millions"; and he bestows a good deal of care on an argument which shows why the New Englander will not settle in New York, New Jersey, or in Pennsylvania. He closes this preface by transporting his hearers to the distance of one hundred years forward from the time in which he speaks. He asks them to look over this wide-spread wilderness of New England, "to see it blossom like the rose, and behold it planted with churches and temples consecrate to the *pure worship* of the Most High,—when our present plain edifices for public worship shall be succeeded with a nobler species of building, not, indeed, with temples whose colonnades are decked with the gilt busts of angels winged, but temples adorned with all the decent ornaments of the most sublime and august architecture; when divinely resplendent truth shall triumph, and our brethren of the Congregational communion may form a body of SEVEN MILLIONS! A glorious and respectable body this, for TRUTH and LIBERTY! Well might our fathers die with pleasure, and sacrifice their lives with joy, to lay the foundation of such a name, of such a peculiar people, whose numbers so soon increase as the sand of the sea or the stars of heaven, and, what is more, whose God is the Lord."

These sanguine hopes of one of the most far-sighted men who has ever lived in New England were doomed, so far as her population goes, to be disappointed. Far-sighted men will overlook something. In this case, the mathematics of Dr. Stiles did not deceive him. It has proved, indeed, that his figures were curiously correct. What he could not believe was, that any New Englander should ever willingly leave New England. Least of all did Dr. Stiles conceive it possible that many men should go beyond the country of the savage Six Nations, even beyond the "Alleghany Mountain," as Dr. Stiles would have called that range, even beyond the "great river of the West," of which he knew so little, nay even beyond the mountains beyond that river, nay even to the great Southern Sea. With us, the typical New Englander is the man who looks in on everything between pole and pole. But this habit had not shown itself then. The New Englander was still a fisherman and navigator, but he had shown no disposition for distant explorations of the interior. It is true that there is a single tradition, which is probably true, that the men of Massachusetts anticipated La Salle in his discovery of the Mississippi, and that the Indians who led him on this discovery had learned their way under the direction of Massachusetts adventurers. But in the very fact that we cannot wear this laurel, because nobody followed up their discovery, in the fact that for three-quarters of a century France and her Jesuits were left to have their own way in that great valley, is an illustration of the indisposition of our people in general toward inland adventure.

It was not till the Revolutionary War was over that that change came over New England which has resulted in the complete falsification of Ezra Stiles's prophecies. The two wars had given to the new nation the eastern side of the Valley of the Mississippi, as far south as the northern line of Florida. Officers and soldiers who had been discharged from the army found nothing to do at home in the terrible prostration of all trade. Congress was glad enough to pay off its debts to them by grants of land which seem enormous even to our views of land subsidies. Four years after the peace, Manasseh Cutler, a Connecticut minister, led the first colony to Ohio. He covered his emigrant wagon with black canvas on which he painted the words, "Ohio: for Marietta on the Muskingum."

This wagon was the "Mayflower" of the North-west. She started on her voyage only ninety-two years ago. Forty-five men went out with Cutler. You know how the New Englanders have followed their example. That day, they broke their bounds. They passed beyond the Six Nations; they crossed the head waters of the Ohio; they began on that system of penetration of every corner of every valley in this continent, which at this moment gives you a graduate of Harvard College for your host, though you be botanizing in Alaska, or hangs a picture of the Charter Oak over your head as you lie in bed in a cabin in Colorado.

There is no doubt that the leaders of New England at home looked with anxiety on this westward drift. The bitter aversion to the acquisition of Louisiana by the United States was due, in part at least, to such anxiety. When my father was in college, the Philotechnic Society, to which he belonged, discussed in 1803 the question, "Whether the acquisition of Louisiana would be an advantage to the United States? Decided in the negative." I think the vote was 34 to 5. In a pamphlet published in 1804, the writer uses the following language: ... "The settlement of our new lands will be discouraged by allurements to regions of greater promise and fertility.

"The men naturally destined to populate the District of Maine, the vacant lands of New Hampshire and Vermont, will be enticed to the new paradise of Louisiana, which, after a few more jubilees, will throw off its allegiance to a government too distant to compel obedience, and unite with a country beyond the Alleghany in the dismemberment of the nation. The sinews of New England will be drawn out to invigorate new settlements in countries which God and Nature have made it impossible to unite under one government for a length of time; and *our monies* will be expended on post roads, which, for years to come, must be chiefly traversed by wolves and catamounts. But these mischiefs, however fatal, and accompanied as they probably will be by a substitution of philosophical whims for national establishments, are the least which will result from the supremacy of one State over the rest."

WHERE ARE THE NEW ENGLANDERS?

There can be little doubt that Dr. Stiles's estimate of the future growth of the New England population was correct, and that there are now living many more than eight million persons who descend from the twenty-two thousand who emigrated from England under the lead of the Puritan Fathers; only these millions of people are not cooped up, as he supposed they would be, within the confines of New England. There are, I am told, and I believe, more men and women of New England blood in San Francisco than there are in Boston. There are undoubtedly more persons of New England origin in Ohio than in Connecticut. Nothing is more curious or suggestive than the census tables which show the diffusion over every State of the persons born in New England. Yet these tables do not show the descendants in the second and after generations. Of these eight millions of Dr. Stiles's estimate, which was as I suppose correct, probably not two millions live in the three States which he assigned as the home for eight in 1860. The other millions are scattered over all parts of this land, and other regions of the world.

THE WORLD'S ADVANCE.

The increase of population, thus proceeding by general laws, of which Dr. Stiles understood the formula, gives no hint of the increase of wealth, comfort, refinement; of the change in social order and home life; of the advance in education, in philosophy, and the arts of life, especially in civil order and in religion, which these hundred and twenty years have made. Nothing is more amusing than the braggart boasting of our American oratory,— its congratulations on what has been achieved. The most amusing feature often is, that the orator is a person who has done nothing himself towards the advancement which he proclaims. But no prophet of our future ever succeeds in portraying, in advance, either the method or rapidity of its progress. I happened, in early life, to see, every day, the men who, in face of the derision of the solid men of their time, were forcing the railroad system upon unwilling Massachusetts. It is not fifty years since those days. Well, in their wildest dreams of the future, there was not a man of them who looked forward to the development which we see to-day. I remember that in a speech at Faneuil Hall, my father based his estimates on a daily travel of nine persons each way between Boston and Connecticut River, and with what pleasure he told us, on his return, that the audience cried out that this was not large enough. I have the manuscript journal of one of the finest young men of New England, in which he describes with rage the sight of a cotton factory in Waltham. He looked with horror on that cruel Moloch of machinery which was, as he supposed, to be the ruin of our laboring men! For such reasons, there is no more instructive reading than a volume of the pamphlets of fifty years ago. Whatever they prophesy of evil — and of course they prophesy evil — is evil which has not come. Whatever they prophesy of good does not approach the level which has been attained. There is not the man of us, nor the woman, who has foresight enough to tell what will be the discoveries of the next ten years, nor broad enough, even if he knew them, to multiply into each other the results of these discoveries, and give to us their product as it will show itself in our civilization. And there is no one, whatever his enthusiasm for human nature, who is able to prophesy what the man of the future can do, when he shall have armor, weapons, and tools wrought out by new science in new fields, and so achieving victories now wholly unknown. Yet we are as wise as our fathers. In such ignorance as ours, then, we can see why it was that they have never, at any moment, been able to forecast the future, of which we are.

Let me say this, too, in passing: that New England has gone through more than one fundamental change in her social order in this period of one hundred and twenty years. Dr. Stiles spoke to the representatives of three colonies, who were on the eve of paying their congratulations to the young prince, George III., who that year came to the throne. There were not more loyal men in the British empire,—indeed, it would be hard to find any who expressed their loyalty with that sort of fervor that belonged to the provincialism of colonists. That generation had not passed, Dr. Stiles himself was not dead, before these very men were at work framing new constitutions of government for independent States, and laying the foundation on which this nation stands to-day. Or, take it in the appliances of physical life; take it in matters of business: Dr. Stiles spoke to men whose wealth was gathered from the seas in their fisheries, or in the commerce which they maintained with the various shores of the Atlantic. A generation had not passed before these men and their sons were carrying on the trade of the new-born nation with the East Indies and with the North-west Coast; and in a few years more they were at the head of the carrying trade of the world. Various causes, among which the sullen jealousy of the Southern States of America was foremost, crippled that trade, and in the end broke it up for years. The young Hotspurs of the South and West, under the lead of Calhoun and Clay, who were joined in this policy, meant to punish poor New England by the destruction of her commerce. Poor New England took them at their word, and built up that system of manufacture which makes the New England of to-day, of which Mr. Calhoun lived to be more jealous than ever the hottest Hotspur of his young companions was of her foreign trade. From fishermen and sailors, our people became, without knowing it, the manufacturers for this nation, and you know for how much of the rest of the world. Such have been the changes in politics and in business; as for the change in education and religion, I need not speak. There is a satisfaction in saying that some men, as Stiles did in this very address, boldly prophesied the improvement in theology which is now matter of history, and claimed wisely that in the Congregational order there was always room for more light proceeding from God's holy word.

There has been no incident of these miraculous changes more curious than that in which New England, for half a century, provided the men and women for the higher education for all parts of this country. She sent out the schoolmasters and the school-mistresses of the South and the West. The Western colleges were founded by her sons, and their first professors were educated in her schools. It is not fifty years agó that Mr. Calhoun said, in conversation, that he had seen the time, when, in the House of Representatives in Congress, the natives of Connecticut and the graduates of Yale College in Connecticut made nearly one-half of the

House, lacking only five of an actual majority. Yet at no time, I suppose, has the population of Connecticut been more than one-thirtieth part of the United States. It is twenty years ago that a French traveller, sent here on a mission by the French Government, called my attention to the system by which, as he said, Massachusetts and Connecticut educated the United States. "I have been through Canada," said he, "and through your Western States. In every State, I have found that the teachers of the schools were from Massachusetts or Connecticut. The thing is without parallel in history. There has never been a land of which it could be said that the teachers were all from the same province. I have inquired," said he, "for the statistics, that I might include them in my report to government. I have found that no one could give them to me. I have said 'When I come as far as Massachusetts, I shall find them proud of this. I can obtain these statistics there.' And now I have come here," he said, "no one knows anything about it." I encouraged him by telling him that without giving the full statistics I could obtain some details which would illustrate what he wanted. And when I next saw our dear friend, Dr. Joseph Allen, the minister of Northboro', I asked him how many of their young people who had gone West in forty years had become teachers. He seemed surprised that I should ask such a simple question, and his answer was, "Practically all of them." The simple truth is, that, in one capacity or another, every man or woman who goes into the North-west from New England devotes himself to the maintenance of a high standard of public education. And you know the consequence. The school systems of the North-west are quite as good as yours, and so is their administration. As for school-houses, they had the advantage of the liberality, more than princely, of the general government, which gave to them one-sixteenth of the proceeds of the land sales. And so, in those States which had the wisdom to use this fund for their school-houses, you may see, in towns which are only five years from prairie, school-houses as good as you have in Boston,— much better than the average district school-house of New England.

As I see Western men and men from the Pacific, though I find they may be willing to make fun of Yankee peculiarities, I never find them ashamed of Yankee blood, or unwilling to claim relationship when they can. New England is proving her likeness to Old England, as she sends out her colonies over the world. As the England of the "tight little island" sends her books, her inventions, her tools, her drumbeat, and her sons and daughters to Canada, to Australia, to New Zealand, to the Cape, and to India, so does this other England, this New England, send out her children. I do not see but that they are as loyal to their mother. And it is truly in their lives that she lives.

HOW NEW ENGLAND SHALL RETAIN HER ASCENDANCY.

But if she wishes to maintain this ascendancy, it must be by the same means which won it. She must send out her people, not one by one to take their chances of being absorbed and overpowered by their new neighbors, but in companies of men and women able and willing to bear each others' burdens. I say companies of men and women. It is the earliest distinction of New England, and one of the greatest, that the Pilgrim Fathers invented this system of colonizing. They builded better than they knew in this, as in so many other things. The foundations of Manhattan were laid by men alone, eager to go home as soon as their engagement closed. So at Jamestown in Virginia, the first settlers were all men. Farther back yet, the unsuccessful colony of Popham was a colony of men. It would be fair to call the modern system in which the men who rule a colony go as a part of it, and go with their women and children, all determined to remain, "the New England system."

It is by such colonies, carrying with them, from the first, home, church, school, and every other requisite of society, that the power of any State extends itself. 'It was thus that Greece multiplied herself in the larger Greece, and Rome in the colonies which maintained the Roman Empire. Let your New Englander go alone — nay, let him go with his wife and little ones — into Virginia, into 'Mississippi, into Louisiana, all of which are begging him to come. The chances are that he is back again in twelve months. His wife is homesick, — he is discouraged. They laughed at him because he spoke through his nose. They were glad of his money, but they did not like his company. And she had been an outcast in her own land. 'But let forty of those families go together. Let them open their district school the day after their arrival. Let them hold their meeting on their first "Sabbath" under a live-oak tree. Let them sing the songs of the Lord in the strange land, and at night let them come together to tell the old stories and to dream the old dreams. Then they carry victory with them. Not to go back to Cutler's settlement of Marietta, or to the early histories of the Western Reserve, our own time gives noble illustration of such successes. It was such organization of emigration which made Kansas the State she is. It is but twenty-five years this summer that the first settler was admitted there. In those early years, not many more than two thousand persons from New England went in there,— but they were picked men and women. They went with a principle to sustain. And they were organized from the beginning.

That was the power which made the infant colony to be the rock upon which broke the wave of extending slavery. "Thus far shalt thou come, and no farther." Fourteen years ago, the same experiment was repeated in Florida more quietly. The same Company which had led in the settlement of Kansas gave the information and advice which sent into Florida several thousand emigrants from the North-east and the North-west. No other State of the "Confederacy" received such an infusion of Northern blood. And that is the reason why in the election of two years ago Florida threw her weight into the Northern scale.

Such experiments cannot be too carefully considered. The New Englander alone, is as helpless as any other man alone. If he is to carry with him the talisman which has made his home the home he loves, he must carry with him that home in institutions and organizations. He must carry the tabernacle and the shrine and the Holy of Holies as he has seen it in the mount, if he would not have his children seeking for strange gods, and false, forgetting the glories of Zion.

And these illustrations suggest to us what is to be the true future of New England, if she is to have any. This little cluster of States may soon be left out in the cold,— outnumbered, out-voted, stripped and peeled by States which she has beaten into submission and then replaced with honor in the national councils. But, as there are other Englands in New Zealand, in Australia, and in India, so there are other New Englands in Michigan, in Iowa, in Kansas, in Oregon, and in California; and there may be others, if you and I, and others like us, choose, in Texas and New Mexico, in Florida,— yes, and in South Carolina. As this dreary winter has gone by, I have had, day after day in my office, different groups of five or six young men each, haggard and weary with doing nothing, who had come in one by one to ask me where they should go, and what they could do. Such sense of power still attaches to the Christian Church, that men still look to its ministers to work miracles where all other means have failed. Every such day, I have said to myself what I could not say to them, Where is the Miltiades, where is the John Winthrop, where is the Manasseh Cutler, where is the Charles Robinson, to unite you together, and with you to found a new State? Where is the young gentleman of honor, of courage, and of energy enough to do what those men knew how to do, and marshal together these who are powerless to go alone? We do a great thing when we plant a college in the West, like Antioch or Oberlin. We give the West priceless treasure when we send to them our best blood, our children, one by one or two by two. But we build up our own future, we secure that supremacy of New England in this nation which this nation must enjoy if it is to live, when we send our sons and daughters,— not alone but in companies.

Such a State as Texas is to have more physical weight in this empire of ours than all these six States of New England. It is for us and our children to see that this physical force is swayed by moral power; and this is only one illustration. You heard here the message which Utah sends you, and that lovely valley of New Mexico, just now swayed by Jesuits. Another day, the message is from the Indian Territory. And each new day has its different tale. It is as she answers such appeals, or as she falls back lazily to sleep under her old-time laurels, that New England is to win her victories of the future, or to be left in history an old-time name and a respected memory.

www.ingramcontent.com/pod-product-compliance
Lightning Source LLC
Chambersburg PA
CBHW030308170426
43202CB00009B/920